TRAILBLAZING SPORTS HEROES

AMAZING STORIES

TRAILBLAZING SPORTS HEROES

Exceptional Personalities and Outstanding
Achievements in Canadian Sport

HISTORY/SPORT

by Joan Dixon

PUBLISHED BY ALTITUDE PUBLISHING CANADA LTD.
1500 Railway Avenue, Canmore, Alberta T1W 1P6
www.altitudepublishing.com
1-800-957-6888

Extreme care has been taken to ensure that all information presented in
this book is accurate and up to date. Neither the author nor the
publisher can be held responsible for any errors.

Publisher	Stephen Hutchings
Associate Publisher	Kara Turner
Editor	Jill Foran

We acknowledge the financial support of the Government
of Canada through the Book Publishing Industry Development
Program (BPIDP) for our publishing activities.

Altitude GreenTree Program
Altitude Publishing will plant twice as many trees as were used
in the manufacturing of this product.

National Library of Canada Cataloguing in Publication Data

Dixon, Joan
Trailblazing Sports Heroes / Joan Dixon

(Amazing stories)
Includes bibliographical references.
ISBN 1-55153-976-4

1.
I. Title. II. Series: Amazing stories (Canmore, Alta.)

Printed and bound in Canada by Friesens
2 4 6 8 9 7 5 3 1

Cover: Tom Longboat sprints for the line
(Reproduced courtesy of Canada's Sports Hall of Fame)

To the sporting life!

Bobbie Rosenfeld

Contents

Prologue

It was November 15, 1880, and Ned Hanlan was looking out at the crowd that had gathered along the banks of the Thames to see him race. Spotting a few fans and newspaper reporters among the swarm, he suddenly felt the need to say a few words. "I can assure you I will do my best," he said, "not only for myself and friends but for the honour of the country across the water, which I love so well."

Ned reviewed his preparations once again. His body felt tuned, his boat intact, and his strategy composed. He had rowed this race a thousand times in his mind; he couldn't be more ready. Glancing over at the rowing shell beside him, he saw his competitor take off his jersey and show off his gigantic frame and bulging muscles. The crowd roared.

But Ned could hear a few friendly voices shouting out to him as well.

"Best of luck, little Canuck!"

"Go, Boy in Blue!"

Over 100,000 people had gathered along the

riverbanks to watch this "race of the century." Ned's opponent was a boastful, powerful-looking rower who had prematurely proclaimed himself world champion. Ned, for one, could not allow this conceit. He was there today to show the world that Canadians, too, could be masters of the waterways.

Those betting on the race were not all so sure. Ned had been sorely harassed all week. His opponent's supporters had insulted his small stature and laughed at his unusual stroke. His training sessions on the river had been routinely interrupted with taunts and trickery. Someone had even tried to tamper with his boat while he slept. Of course, Ned wasn't all that surprised. After all, there was both big money and national pride resting on this important race, the first world championship in history.

Ned had endured all the shenanigans and had not stooped to respond. He knew he would have his chance for reply on the water. His plan today was to establish Canadian superiority without a doubt.

Ned Hanlan
Canada's First World Champion

*"As if propelled by magic grace
his boat was foremost in the race"*
1926 poem dedicated to Ned Hanlan

I t was 1867, the year of Confederation, and 12-year-old Edward "Ned" Hanlan was pulling hard on his oars, groaning from the exertion. He couldn't be late for school, but his rowboat was still a couple of kilometres from the Toronto mainland. Finally, the undersized boy found a rhythm that let him drift into a daydream. He imagined he was one of the underdog Canadian rowers who had just recently competed at the World's Fair in Paris. The "Paris Crew," as the Canadian rowers became known, was a ragtag bunch of Maritime fishermen who rowed together in an old-fashioned boat. They had been sent to represent the country in its first international rowing competition. And, while they may have looked out of place in their pink caps and leather suspenders, they had managed to defeat the English and European favourites, all of whom rowed in sleek boats and stylish uniforms. Inspired by the Paris Crew's victory, Ned made it to shore in record time. Turning his daily commute to school into a race always helped speed him up.

In Canada, rowing had just recently evolved from transportation to sport, but it was quickly becoming popular with both participants and spectators. Ned Hanlan was only one of the Paris Crew's many Canadian followers who were more interested in hearing news about the rowing race than about Confederation. Having spent all of his childhood living on an island, rowing was as familiar to Ned as walking. The son of an Irish immigrant and fisherman who had settled on Toronto Island, Ned grew up with oars in his hands. He was barely five years old when he first managed the feat of rowing across the harbour to the city of Toronto, his preparation for a lifetime on the water.

Ned didn't know it then, but he would later become one of the first athletes to use rowing as his ticket out of the working class. First, though, he had to follow in his father's wake, rowing as a fisherman's helper. It was good training. When he had time, he also rowed in competitions. Canada was a little more democratic in its ideas about amateur and professional athletes than England was in the mid 1800s. In England, anybody who did manual or menial labour (including rowing as a fisherman's helper) was barred from amateur rowing races. But in Canada, rowing was a sport where the class divisions of the time could blend. Professional and amateur racers were not always separated until the 1880s.

At 16, Ned successfully tested his natural gift in his first public competition, a fisherman's race. Two years later, he was able to race in a real racing shell — as long, narrow, and lightweight as his rowboat was short, wide, and heavy — for the first time. In 1873, at the age of 18, he won the amateur championship of Toronto Bay. Amateur rowers, mostly members of the upper class who rowed for recreation, earned only trophies for their successes. When Ned went on to beat well-known rower Tom Louden, Louden wanted a rematch against the newcomer. As an indication of how serious and confident he was, Louden backed up his challenge with a side bet of $100. Motivated by this new benefit in rowing, Ned agreed to the rematch, and won again. Betting wins aside, Ned soon realized that if he wanted to make a real living out of his natural abilities, he would have to race as a bona fide professional in the rapidly growing commercial part of rowing. He couldn't do that without help.

Fortunately, Ned's early successes had attracted notice from the "money men" of rowing. By then, rowing had become Canada's most popular spectator sport because it was exciting to watch and bet on. The Hanlan Club was formed by a group of upstanding citizens in the Toronto community who wanted to invest in Ned's — and Canada's — future sporting success. Ned's backers planned to one day "set him on his way to the English Crown," which was the dream of all aspiring rowers in the British Empire. England was not only the ancestral home of rowing, but also of most Ontarians. The club would arrange Ned's equipment and matches, and also protect him from the potential of bribery and corruption, the darker parts of the sport.

As a professional backed by the Hanlan Club, Ned could now also collect money for his talent. At 20, he won his first $100 prize in a local race. His club was so impressed with his easy win that they set him up for an international race in the United States. He would compete at the Centennial Regatta in Philadelphia.

But first he had to get out of trouble. Right before Ned was to leave for Philadelphia, the Toronto police issued a warrant for his arrest. To make money when he wasn't racing or fishing, Ned had been bootlegging — illegally selling alcohol — near his family's hotel on the Island. Wanting very much to avoid arrest, he tried hiding out for a couple of days, but the police eventually chased him to the waterfront and into his rowing club. As the constables came through the front doors of the clubhouse to arrest him, the quick-thinking Ned managed to sneak out the back way to the dock. He commandeered a boat and rowed away at full speed. Club members and bystanders couldn't help but cheer for the underdog. Ned rowed harder, buoyed by the support. Across the lake, a steamer happened to be passing by on its way to the United States. Someone on the ship, seeing the chase, lowered a rope ladder, and Ned climbed to safety. On board, he waved cheekily to the police on the shoreline and basked in the attention.

His club arranged for Ned's shell and trainer to meet him at the American regatta. The warm-up on the way there must have buoyed the novice racer; Ned surprised everyone by beating the most experienced rowers in the United States and two top British ones. Instead of the police, the whole of Toronto greeted Ned on his return home with marching bands, rockets, and a torchlight parade. Suddenly, all criminal charges against him were forgotten. With his dark, fashionably curly hair and intense eyes, the young rascal had endeared

Ned Hanlan was the first to master the
new sliding seat and extendable oarlocks.

himself to the public. No one knew what this newcomer
would do next, but they would certainly pay attention.

In 1879, the Hanlan Club decided Ned was ready to
challenge the mother country. By then, Ned had won
both the Canadian and American rowing championships, as well as a tremendous following. The English
rowing fraternity still doubted that it was possible for
the "colonies" to produce better rowers than the

"masters of the waterways." But Ned, who always raced in the blue colours of the Hanlan Club, would soon prove them wrong.

Ned won the English championship by 11 boat lengths and in a time 55 seconds faster than the record. The English masters were aghast at his stroke technique, claiming "everything was wrong with it except the results." They had to concede, however, Ned's mastery of the new technology. He was the first they had seen to efficiently use the sliding seat on runners. Most other rowers still found the new device a nuisance. But the sliding seat and extendable roll-locks extended the short man's stroke and gave him an advantage. Ned rowed so evenly and smoothly in his races that people watching remarked, "his boat seemed to be pulled through water on a string."

After Ned's 1879 win, reporters from England, the United States, and Canada mobbed him. One reporter asked, "As the holder of the three titles, Canadian, American, and English, what nationality do you consider yourself?" Not missing a beat, Ned proudly replied, "I am a Canadian." The Hanlan Club was ecstatic with the achievement of their goal. "[Ned's] victories in England have done more than all the advertising and emigration agents in the past combined to make known the position and power of the Dominion of Canada."

Ned Hanlan's next race was billed as the event of the century by the rowing-crazed newspapers. He had challenged the famous Edward Trickett, an Australian rower who had arrogantly and prematurely proclaimed himself world champion because he had recently beaten England's top rower. Before the Olympic Games were revived in 1896, athletes in other sports would rarely travel for competition outside their country. The difficulties of time restriction and transportation prevented it. As a result, this world championship of rowing would be the first and only world championship of any sport at the time. The race was set for November 15, 1880, and would take place in England because Trickett refused to compete in North America. The River Thames in London would be the site of the contest.

With the confidence of a nation on his small, wiry shoulders, Ned travelled to England and prepared for the race in his usual way. As he trained throughout the week leading up the race, he found it increasingly difficult to avoid and ignore his competitor, Trickett, whom he had found to be "a bit of a blowhard." Ned nevertheless stuck doggedly to his routine, a strenuous one by most standards.

Before breakfast every day, Ned walked briskly for five kilometres around cold, damp London to warm up his muscles. After a short rest, he and his coach would train on the river. Ned kept his first workout of the day at a "moderate" speed so that he could familiarize himself with the course and spot swift currents or potential obstacles. His pace often drew jeers and insults from Trickett's scouts on the shore. Trickett's supporters perhaps didn't realize that Ned was holding back, and he didn't bother to enlighten them. Instead, he left them all behind at the river and went off to enjoy the next part of his daily routine: a massage and a hot shower. Ned also liked to have time to read the paper or chat with his own supporters who had travelled to England to watch the race.

At exactly noon every day, Ned ate his usual lean steak and stale bread. He chased the meal down with a glass of Scotch ale — to help his digestion, he claimed. Whether due to the morning workout or the ale, he always needed an hour's rest before he went out for his next, longer walk. After a rubdown, his second workout of the day took place at the racecourse. First he rowed at half speed, then he increased his stroke rate to racing speed. Meanwhile, Trickett's friends would try out all sorts of tactics to intimidate him. At this point in his professional career, Ned was quite used to the rowing sport's shenanigans, which were often designed to influence the betting odds before the race. Trickett's supporters, however, were especially irritating. They set up false obstacles on the course and arranged for other boats to interfere with Ned's training route. Ned's trainers even had to be vigilant about his shell to protect it from attempts at vandalism. By nine o'clock every night, the weary athlete was ready for a good 10-hour sleep and dreams of revenge on the racecourse.

On the morning of the contest, cold misty showers did not prevent huge crowds of rowdy spectators from lining up alongside the seven-kilometre racecourse. Newspaper reports counted at least 100,000 people jostling their umbrellas on the banks of the river. To get the best view of the rowing "colonials" from Canada and Australia, the spectators spilled out into boats and onto the bridges that crossed the Thames. Most of them had bets on one rower or the other. Rowing fans who weren't able to be there in person waited outside telegraph and newspaper offices across the Empire for word on the race's progress. Even Canada's Governor General, Lord Lorne, was standing by for the results.

Back on the water, the two athletes were getting ready to race. Dressed in his trademark blue shirt and shorts, Ned looked tiny next to Trickett, who was over six feet four inches tall and weighed almost 200 pounds. Standing almost a foot shorter and weighing only 155 pounds, Ned hardly resembled a professional rower. Yet despite his apparent physical disadvantage, he appeared cool and composed, chewing on a toothpick while waiting for the starter's signal. Trickett, on the other hand, looked taut, his eyes hollow and lips drawn tightly. Despite his physical bearing and his incessant boasting throughout the week, he wasn't the clear favourite by race day.

About $100,000 worth of wagers ($10–20 million in today's dollars) rested on this single race. Strategy was as important as strength in rowing, and Ned knew his unusual pacing of races had previously served him well. He knew when to pull hard and when to rest, and he used his flawless technique to make his races look easy. In only one race had he ever tried to get to the finish line in the fastest possible time. During that race, his only opponent had been the clock, and his amazing time stood unbeaten for more than 100 years!

Around noon, the fog lifted and the River Thames reappeared, smooth and clear — perfect conditions for rowing. The starter's shout triggered the two sets of oars into the water, and the excited crowd swelled in anticipation of a close race. People could see that both rowers were using the sliding seats and extendable oarlocks. Who would prevail? The blades of both rowers entered the water precisely and rhythmically, in mesmerizing repetition. Trickett began with a short stroke that depended on the power of his muscular arms and he took the lead right away. However, Ned's steady knees-to-nose stroke soon countered. His oars appeared to be just tapping the water, but at the moment the blades gripped, Ned's strong legs drove the seat towards the bow of his boat, pushing it forward powerfully. By one and a half kilometres, Ned had pulled ahead two boat lengths. Perhaps he found the cheering from the crowd distracting because all of a sudden he steered off course slightly. His fans and he knew that he couldn't afford to run aground there or anywhere else on the swift section. But it was a momentary lapse and Ned soon compensated.

By the first bridge, one third of the way down the course, Ned had gained another boat length in lead. People clambered all over the bridge to get the best view of his boat coming out from the other side. Seconds passed and no boat appeared. The noise of the crowd died down. Rowing with his back to the course, Trickett had to check over his shoulder to see what had happened to silence the spectators. Finally, the confident Ned emerged from under the bridge, leaning back leisurely in his shell. He'd had a good rest, and, figuring he could afford it, was now lazily paddling first with one oar then the other. Trickett couldn't see the mischievous grin on Ned's face, so he continued to row frantically to catch up. Just as a huffing Trickett pulled even, Ned picked up his oars and the pace. With a wink at the spectators standing nearby, he took off in the lead again. Trickett scowled and tensely rowed on.

Before the halfway point, about 15 minutes into the race, Ned looked a little bored. He stopped again, and this time took the opportunity to scan the spectators. Finally, he spotted someone he knew watching from a shell nearby — the one-time English champion whom he had beaten just the year before. Ned rowed over to the other boat for a chat, as if he was merely in a training session. Not familiar with Ned's strategies of pacing, the crowd was stirred into a frenzy as Trickett started to catch up to him. Ned paused in his conversation to check Trickett's position, then dipped a hand into the river and leisurely wet his face. Refreshed, he returned to his race lane and continued on. Up ahead were the headquarters of the Canadian contingent, so Ned stopped once more to take off his handkerchief and wave it at his Canadian supporters. With only one and a half kilometres to go, Ned resumed his lead of three boat lengths, despite a frustrated Trickett rowing steadily the whole time. At this point, the people on the banks must have thought the race was over. Ned was so close to the finish line that he was sure to win.

But the race wasn't over yet. With only 500 metres to go, Ned suddenly collapsed. He slumped forward in his gliding boat, his oars drifting uselessly. Hearing the crowds' collective gasp, Trickett was forced to turn around again. With the renewed hope of a pardoned man, he pulled out his remaining reserves. "What happened to Ned?" bewildered voices in the crowd cried. Perhaps his fast start and tomfoolery had worn him out, leaving nothing for the end. Trickett had almost reached the Hanlan shell when Ned suddenly jumped upright. He flashed his engaging smile to the crowd once more and then sped off. The roar of laughter from the surrounding spectators took a long time to die down. The amusing rower had done it again. Even those who had bet on Trickett couldn't help but admire the skill and confidence of a true competitor. But Ned wasn't quite finished his clowning. He still wanted to pay the Australian back for his earlier cockiness. The boy in blue zigzagged all the way to the finish line, pulling with one oar then the other. Cannons, bells, and whistles greeted the new world champion and chased a humiliated Trickett off to hide from his outraged countrymen. Later, a special fund had to be started to help return Trickett's broke and stranded Australian supporters to their own country. They'd lost all their money betting on his victory.

Ned's own countrymen celebrated his triumph in high style. A Canadian newspaper article that was published the day after the race reported that it was nearly impossible for a "patriotic Canadian however much he may regret the wild gambling exhibitions connected with yesterday's famous race not to feel proud of Hanlan's splendid performance." Everyone in the English speaking world now knew of Canada's "Boy in Blue." Years after he retired from racing, Ned's popularity still rivalled that of the well-loved Prime Minister Wilfred Laurier.

Ned retained his world title for four more years. His sport, however, was quickly becoming tainted by increasing controversies and scandals over betting and prize monies. But because of his undeniable talents in rowing, Ned's own reputation did not suffer along with the sport. Even at the end of his career, when he was no longer winning, people would still travel to see him row. Soon after Ned retired, officials in the sport decided to separate the professionals who rowed for a living from the amateurs who were interested in fair competition for the fun of it. Most Canadians were not yet comfortable with sportsmen playing for the sake of money. Consequently, the crowds stayed home, yearning for the skillful Ned Hanlan, who had transformed the sport into entertainment worth watching.

By 1900, rowing had become mostly amateur again, attracting more participants than spectators. Ned worked as a rowing coach for a while then later became an outspoken Toronto politician working on behalf of the underdog. He knew he had been lucky to change his future through rowing; most of the working class boys he grew up with never had such an opportunity. Ned continued to be honoured for his athletic accomplishments long after he retired. The world's only statue of a sculler (located at the CNE in Toronto) is dedicated to Ned. Also, one end of Toronto Island, where he grew up, was formally christened Hanlan's Point. As the Dominion of Canada's first individual world champion, the talented and popular Ned Hanlan had truly put his newly formed country on the map.

Tom Longboat
Canada's First
Professional Athlete

"Whenever Tom lined up for a start
He gave his people hope and heart"
Landon Longboat, grandson, age 12

Even the fastest man on earth couldn't run forever. Flashing his trademark grin and tipping his hat at passers-by, 60-year-old Tom Longboat looked fit and content sweeping leaves and collecting rubbish from the streets of Toronto in 1942. For 19 years, he had proudly worked for the city's street cleaning department, first driving a horse and cart, and later a truck. He didn't mind if people thought the job was not good enough for Canada's greatest distance runner. When his running career was over and jobs were scarce during the Depression years, he still needed to support his family. He felt fortunate to be able to walk and work outdoors again. At that time, Tom lived with his family in an upscale residential neighbourhood in the city, about 100 kilometres north-west from the Iroquois Confederacy's Six Nations reserve where he grew up. Native and non-native friends were welcomed equally at his city home despite the racial discrimination and exploitation Tom experienced his whole life. "No sense having a grudge on account of a few inconsiderate people," he always said. Still, even in the 1940s he rarely had to buy himself a drink when he was downtown, though he denied he was still a celebrity. "Oh, I'm not news any more," he claimed, "I've had my day."

Tom's "day" was in the early 1900s, when Canada was proud of its "racing redskin." Running had always been an honoured tradition in Tom's Onandaga heritage, and by the turn of the 20th century, distance running was eclipsing rowing in popularity throughout all of Canada. The longest distance race — the marathon — had been established with the revival of the Olympic Games in 1896. In no time, marathon runners were being treated like modern hockey superstars, and Canada boasted a few of them. At the 1900 Boston Marathon, the most famous of annual distance races,

Canadian athletes swept first, second, and third place. The next year, Jack Caffery won again, and Bill Davis, a Mohawk from Six Nations — and Tom's mentor — came in second.

At the 1907 Boston Marathon, many of the 200,000 spectators were betting on another Canadian. New to racing, Tom Longboat had caught the eye of Bill Davis a few years earlier while playing lacrosse on their reserve. At that time, the only racing Tom had ever done was to win baskets of food at local agricultural fairs. But Bill encouraged Tom to test his natural talents, and his 75-cent rubber sneakers, in a few of the bigger races around Ontario. When Tom managed to upset the favourites two years in a row, he was pronounced ready for Boston. It was a rapid rise to the big leagues for the gangly 19-year-old, and businessmen were quick to volunteer themselves as his managers and bet on his incredible potential.

At noon on April 19, 1907, 124 amateur runners set off from the small town of Ashland, Massachusetts, towards Boston. Near the beginning of the race, the course intersected a railroad track, and Tom barely managed to cross before the freight train did. Runners who weren't quite as fast had to wait long minutes for the train to chug by before they could continue. To ward off the chill of the cool April wind, Tom was still wearing his lucky sweater after the first five kilometres. His head cold was bothering him a little and he wanted to be properly warmed up before he picked up his pace. He could see the high-stepping runners in the pack ahead of him pumping with their elbows. Tom held his arms lower, near his hips, and kicked his feet sideways in such an odd way that people in the crowd couldn't help but shout out comments. Tom just nodded and grinned, as if to say "wait and see." Although it was unorthodox, Tom's style served as an efficient way to conserve his energy for the long race.

When Tom finally did take his sweater off, he threw it to his manager, who was riding beside the course in a slow-moving car. The manager missed the toss, and to everyone's surprise, Tom stopped, casually turned around to pick the sweater up off the road, and tossed it again. He wasn't about to lose his favourite sweater! In the meantime, a dozen more runners passed him. His manager moaned but Tom just grinned. He had everything under control. His long stride, covering almost two metres, was deceptive in its speed. By the halfway point, he was in the lead, breaking the wind for a couple of other runners, one of whom had won the Boston Marathon before. A little later, Tom had only one other runner, Charlie Petch, keeping up with him. The good-looking Tom grinned and waved as a female admirer with a Canadian flag sang out, "Tom Longboat, he'll win." A few kilometres on, at two steep roller coaster hills, Charlie slowed. Tom sped up.

Throughout the last half of the race, a snow squall had been brewing. As well, police were having trouble keeping the eager spectators from getting a closer look at the new star and blocking his path. But nothing would keep Tom from his goal now. Even before he saw the finish line, he broke into a sprint, and finished more than a kilometre ahead of anyone else. He had run the race in two hours, 24 minutes, and 25 seconds, shattering the course record by an astonishing five minutes. Tom accepted his trophy with a shy grin and hurried off to dinner while the rest of the pack was still running.

When he returned home after the race, tens of thousands of fans greeted Tom at the Toronto train station. With the Union Jack flag draped around his shoulders, he rode in an open car in one of the biggest torchlight parades Toronto had ever put on for anyone. Military bands and fireworks accompanied a presentation of the keys to the city. During this ceremony, Tom was also given a gold medal and a promise of money for his education. Overwhelmed, he stood by as his managers gave acceptance speeches; in those days society's majority didn't expect a Native person to have anything intelligent to say anyway.

Back home on the reserve, nobody treated him any differently after his big win, and he liked it that way. There, he was "just Tom," a young man with a smile for everyone. Born June 4, 1882, Tom was five years old when his father died. Though there were several prosperous families on the reserve, the Longboat family lived in a one-room log cabin heated by a wood stove. From their modest little farm, which had just a few chickens and a cow, they eked out a living. The family didn't have a horse, so Tom often had to pull the plough through the field himself. He didn't mind; physical labour outdoors suited him better than the missionary school, which tried to expunge his Native heritage. The school forbade the Longhouse religion, and the Onondaga language. Every minute of instruction was aimed at discouraging what the teachers believed was laziness, a cultural defect in their eyes. When Tom was 12, he ran away from school and never stopped running.

Once he ran 65 kilometres home when he couldn't find his mother at the end of a day in town. Though she had left hours earlier in a wagon, Tom still beat her back. Like most of his friends on the reserve, he ran because it was fun and it was easy. Bill Davis, however, encouraged him to consider it as a career. Tom's mother later recalled his early training: "Tommy practised running for two years on the reservation. He run every morning.

He run every night. He run down to the [race] and get beaten. He came back and run some more. Soon he run five miles easy in twenty-three and a half minutes. Next time we have five mile race here, Tommy win by nearly quarter of mile."

Through his systematic training, Tom had naturally discovered the modern principles of progressive loading and recovery. His body told him what rhythm he needed, allowing his muscles to build strength gradually and surely. He trained by doing a little speed work, lots of light weights, and playing games of handball or squash. Other times he would just walk long distances or take extended rests to recover. Later, when he continued to insist on training this way, his new managers — and the press — called him lazy and stubborn, a "typical Indian who couldn't be relied upon."

After winning the Boston Marathon, Tom was told by his managers that his next goal would be the 1908 Olympics in London, England. He joined 24 other track and field athletes, 13 of them marathoners like him, to be part of the first ever government-sponsored Olympic team. As in the Boston Marathon, the athletes participating in the Olympics all had to be true amateurs, never paid more than their expenses to race. Tom had already been accused of earning money for his managers from his racing, and had been disqualified from the US amateur races. Unlike in Ned Hanlan's rowing days, the casual mixing of amateurs and professionals was no longer tolerated. As a result, Tom's handlers found him jobs as an office messenger boy and cigar seller so he could earn a living until he was famous enough to race professionally and attract paying spectators. His managers had planned a quarter million dollar professional tour for Tom if he won at the Olympics.

Heavy rain had fallen in London the week of the 1908 Olympic marathon race, wetting the newly surfaced racecourse. One runner pronounced that the surface was hard as flint and bound "to wear out shoes." Race day was unbearably hot and humid. Although he hadn't been practising on the course with the others, Tom was heavily favoured. Donning his maple leaf jersey, he joined 58 other runners on the grounds of Windsor Castle to wait for the official start. The royal family had requested that the start be close by, thereby increasing the official length of the marathon forever to 42.2 kilometres. Among the royal spectators were two future kings, Edward VIII and George VI, playing near their elders, who sat on chairs upholstered with scarlet velvet.

Shortly after 2 p.m., the temperature still rising, Princess Mary pressed a buzzer that told the starter to fire his pistol. Tom burst away, hearing the dignified

Tom Longboat at the 1908 Olympic Games in London

royal clapping give way to schoolboy cheers as he approached Eton College just outside the castle. For the first eight kilometres of the race, Tom stayed 90 metres ahead of the frontrunners. He set such a blistering pace in the scorching heat that many runners had to drop out before making it halfway through the course. By the 27-kilometre mark, his only real competition was fellow Canadian Charles Hefferon, an American by the name of John Hayes, and Italian baker Dorando Pietri. The road was so twisty and narrow in spots that the men had to run single file. More runners quit. At 32 kilometres, Tom was in second place under the strong sun when he slowed to a walk. Suddenly, he thrust his arms in the air, staggered, and fell onto the road, quivering. His manager, who happened to be nearby, immediately poured a little champagne (used as a stimulant in those days) into his mouth to revive him. Tom did not revive. His fans were speechless with shock. The medical officer arrived and loaded him into a car to drive him to the stadium, saying, "This man is dead beat. I won't let him go on."

Among the many controversies of the 1908 Olympic marathon was the suggestion that Tom (and others, including Pietri) had been drugged with strychnine. A commonly used stimulant in those days, the colourless, odourless poison could be easily administered without an athlete's knowledge. And unfortunately, the high profile of the Olympics sometimes led athletes and/or managers to bolster their odds of winning — either the race or their bets — by drugging competitors. Drug testing was as yet unheard of, so no proof was found and no one ever admitted to the deed. Tom would only say the extreme heat and the pounding on the new hard surface had "knocked him out."

Although Tom wanted to retire after this near-fiasco, his managers changed his mind for him and declared him officially professional. It was time for him to earn his keep. Tom was bored at his day jobs anyway, and he liked to run. As a professional, he won more races than any of his contemporaries, at every distance. His superb sense of pace and explosive acceleration brought crowds to their feet. Fans also loved to watch him joking and waving at opponents and spectators during his races. In one much-publicized contest in January 1909, he lined up for an indoor race around a track in Madison Square Gardens. His competition was Englishman Alfie Shrubb, who at that time was considered the world's best professional runner, but was not used to races as long as the marathon. A standing-room-only crowd of 12,000 people paid to watch the men run 262 laps, while 14,000 others waited outside the Gardens for results. In Toronto, thousands more stood outside the newspaper building, where continuous updates came direct from the track.

Alfie Shrubb set a fast pace at the beginning of the race, lapping Tom five times in the first 16 kilometres.

The impatient crowd booed Tom. Undeterred, he ignored the spectators and kept to his own rhythm. Eventually, Shrubb had to slow down, and Tom picked up his pace. The crowd cheered as the two runners matched strides for 10 laps. Shrubb's handlers squirted him with seltzer and fed him coffee and wine to spur him on. Tom took in water and only thimblefuls of champagne. At 33 kilometres, Shrubb stopped to change his shoes. Tom, at that point, was still behind by six laps. His fans cheered him on from trackside as Shrubb's trainers screamed at them to get back to their seats. As the race continued, Shrubb slowed to an unsteady walk. With only a kilometre to go, and Tom less than a lap behind, Shrubb staggered off the track. Tom crossed the finish line grinning. The crowds in New York and Toronto went wild. Tom was proclaimed Professional Champion of the World.

He soon found out, however, that being Canada's first official professional champion meant he was little more than a performing seal. His managers dictated when he ran, for how long, and who and where he raced. The public often gave the managers more credit than "the injun" for his successes. His managers also kept most of the earnings from the contests they arranged. Tom had earned $17, 000 in his first three years as a professional, but quickly spent it on his family and friends.

He built his mother a nicer house on the reserve. He also indulged his love for fancy clothes and bought several three-piece suits, high collar shirts, and hats. Then Tom discovered that he had been sold, "just like a race horse, to make money." The contract he had signed with his manager was transferred for a mere $2000 to another man who wanted to take his own cut from Tom's running. Tom rebelled like he had at missionary school and refused to race, saying: "I do not like the idea of doing all the work and somebody else getting all the credit for winning." He was told he was trouble to manage because he "didn't have a white man's business brain." Finally, he bought out his contract and tried to manage himself.

World War I interrupted Tom Longboat's chance to reap any rewards. In an era when Native peoples were not even able to vote, Tom volunteered to serve his country. His enlistment papers registered his trade as "professional runner." Just as his forefathers had used runners for communication during times of war, the British army used runners when radios failed. Tom was assigned the dangerous job of carrying messages between battlefields on foot. Sometimes he had to lead other soldiers to the front lines because he knew the way. Once when he was leading a British general, the poor man couldn't keep up with Tom's pace. The general barked at Tom to slow down, then yelled, "Who do you think I am, Tom Longboat?" The ever-grinning Tom quickly replied, "No sir, that's me." For much of the war, Tom was also assigned to the Sportsmen's battalion, entertaining the troops with (free) running exhibitions and races.

When the war was over, Tom returned home and, like many other vets, had trouble regaining his old life. Distance running was losing its popularity by then, and Tom had turned 30. He tried his hand at many jobs, including farming out west, but he still had to pawn his medals to get by. Finally, he returned to the east and eventually found work with the city that had given him its keys after his Boston victory. He only raced once more — in an exhibition race of old-timers. At a time when many people couldn't afford a bus ticket, Tom was able to drive off with the prize: a second-hand car.

Tom eventually retired from his street cleaning job in Toronto and moved back to the reserve. He still liked to walk 20 kilometres most days. Never expressing the bitterness others felt on his behalf, he was an inspiration to his people, and was celebrated for sticking to his own ways. Recalled one of his friends, "He was the best in the world, and an Indian besides." His son added, "none of us Longhouse people have to name a building after my father to remember him."

James Naismith & the Edmonton Grads
Canada's Wonder Team

"Nations may totter and politicians rave
Great issues may hang in the balance
And even the end of the world may be in sight
But what does it matter?
The Grads are playing tonight."
May Totter, *Edmonton Journal*, June 1,1935

Canadian James Naismith was filled with apprehension the first time he went to watch the Edmonton Grads play basketball. It had been 34 years since he'd invented the game, and he had been honoured with an invitation to attend the 1925 North American Women's Championships. Typical of men of his era, he had reservations about girls playing any vigorous game. But as he watched the Grads play against Oklahoma's Guthrie Redbirds, he noticed that the Canadian girls were barely letting the other team touch the ball. Jump ball pass from the centre toss, then low pass to bounce pass, another low pass and swish, into the basket; the Grads' rapid tempo was hypnotizing their taller opponents. Naismith also couldn't help but notice the Grads' uncanny ability around the basket. The girls took lots of shots and rarely missed. He couldn't even pick out one dominant player. Dot, Elsie, Mary, Daisy, and captain Connie all played as a unit, constantly and quickly passing as if they always knew exactly where a teammate would be. As the Redbirds started to fade near the end of the game, the Grads continued to showcase their superior fitness.

At stake this day in 1925 was the Underwood Trophy, and it was not the first time the Grads had been challenged for the North American title. The only things that had changed over the last few years were their opponents and their own uniforms. The first time they had won the Underwood (in 1923), they had played in heavy woollen stockings, kneepads, and baggy middies that hung like flour sacks over their knee-length bloomers. Compared to the American players, who had shown up in tight shirts and brief shorts with "WORLD CHAMPS" printed in bold block letters, the Grads had looked ridiculous. At least they had until they'd started to play, at which time they'd quickly demonstrated why their winning record was unparalleled by any team in the history of Canadian sport.

James Naismith was intrigued by the success of the team, and by the increasing popularity of basketball. He had never imagined his game would spread across the world and the sexes. While he had been studying to become a minister at McGill University in the late 1880s, Naismith had shown his fellow students that he was an outstanding athlete. He had been particularly respected for playing sports intensely but always with self-control. One day on the football field, he'd had an epiphany. A teammate had been cursing profusely out of frustration after a botched play, but as soon as he'd noticed that the pious Naismith was standing nearby, he'd stopped and quickly apologized. Naismith had realized then that he could influence mankind just as well on the playing field as he could in a church. Soon after, he signed up to teach physical education at an International YMCA school in Springfield, Massachusetts.

In December of 1891, Naismith was asked to come up with a simple indoor wintertime game to keep his athletes busy and in shape during the off-season. His students loved playing football and soccer, but were bored doing the usual callisthenics and gymnastic drills in the gym while they waited for the snow to melt. When they tried to adapt the game of soccer to the indoors, they ended up with several collisions and a practical lesson in first aid. The resourceful Naismith then tried combining and adapting favourite elements of various ball games. Somehow he had to figure out how to remove any opportunity for body contact — many of the more conservative Christians still called contact sports "tools of the devil."

A game from Naismith's Ontario childhood suddenly resurfaced in memory. Called duck on the rock, the game required an accurate, high arching shot to hit a target. Naismith modified this game by putting a target like a box (or what was handier, a peach basket) not on the ground but up high. This helped eliminate the threat of tackling. Disallowing running with the ball also helped. Passing and team work were to be this game's key features. Not only did Naismith's students catch on to it fast, but the game's popularity also spread throughout the YMCA missionaries. It could be played indoors or out, and it was easy to learn.

Thirty-four years later, in Oklahoma at the North American Underwood match, Naismith could see for himself that the Grads played the game the way he had envisioned it. They rarely fouled and the ball rarely touched the floor. The girls only bounced the ball when they could not throw it, and Naismith was pleased. He thought the one big adaptation to the game — bouncing or dribbling the ball — was a fancy, look-at-me way of playing, and not at all suited to the Grads' team style. It had been an accidental addition to the game anyway, adopted once players discovered it as a way of passing to oneself. Dribbling meant players could run with the ball and risk the body contact that Naismith had tried hard to preclude.

During half-time intermission at the Grads–Redbirds game, Naismith was invited to say a few words. First, he consoled the Oklahoma team and its fans, insisting that there would be no disgrace in losing to the Grads. "I never expected the day when girls could play basketball as these Canadian girls play it. In my opinion, the Grads have the finest basketball team that ever stepped on the floor. I doubt they have any equal in all round strategy, brilliance of play, and doggedness of attack."

He also complimented his new friend, Grads coach Percy Page, for putting his reservations to rest. "To see young ladies exhibiting as much grace and poise at an afternoon tea as vigorous ability on a basketball court, I must credit ... your obvious high standards of sports-manship and coaching." Naismith and Page were kin-dred spirits indeed. Naismith later called Page, "the most superb sportsman it has ever been my good fortune to meet."

Mr. Page, as the ladies always called him, had been a mild mannered 25 -year-old when he'd arrived from Ontario to teach business classes at Edmonton's McDougall Commercial High School. He had played and coached basketball back in Ontario and, like Naismith, considered it a fine game to encourage healthy living habits.

In 1915, Page began to coach his pioneer basketball team of six girls at Commercial High; the team had just joined the brand new Edmonton high school league. Without a gymnasium at their school, they had to play all their home games on an outdoor cinder court. Often winning games by only a point or two, the girls sur-prised even themselves when they won the league. They had so much fun that first year that they begged Mr. Page to continue coaching them, even after graduation. Page agreed to form a club, the Commercial Graduates Basketball Club, whose team became known as the Grads. In semi-weekly practices of 90 minutes, Page patiently and quietly stressed the basics and focussed on teamwork and commitment. He used to tell them, "you must play basketball, think basketball, and dream basketball." But he also reminded them, "you are ladies first and basketball players second and if you can't win playing a clean game, you don't deserve to win." He never raised his voice. The most serious rebuke his girls would ever hear was "tsk, tsk." Like Naismith, he led by example.

Percy Page, in spite of his full-time responsibilities as principal of the high school, was the most dedicated of volunteer coaches. He acted as team manager, too, setting up a development system of junior "Gradettes" to feed the continuing success of the club. After consistently winning the city and provincial championships against high school, university, and their own Gradette teams, Page's Grads had to start looking farther afield for competition. Without his organizational and fundraising efforts, the Grads wouldn't have been able to afford to play. As they attracted more fans, the team moved to the Edmonton Arena, where Page had had a new hardwood floor installed. In their new home, they could now sell more tickets for their games; 25 cents snagged a child a seat in a special section, and a dollar bought a box seat. The Grads were strictly amateurs, with full-time jobs as secretaries, teachers, or clerks; the money from the tickets paid their expenses for out-of-town competitions.

In 1922, each Grad had to contribute $25 to take the train to London, Ontario, where they would play in the first Canadian women's basketball championships. The girls couldn't afford to bring substitute players, and they packed lunches to avoid dining car expenses. When they returned from their journey victorious, almost all the citizens of Edmonton came out to cheer the motorcade carrying the six women down Jasper Avenue. The women received special medals from Mayor David Duggan. They became the toast of Edmonton for their successes, and for the way they represented the city and women in general — with decorum and class.

After the triumphant trip east, the team dared to adopt "boys' rules," which allowed for a wide-open game with more running and checking, and required five players instead of six. The Grads believed that the "girls' rules" virtually eliminated the normal flow of the game. The rules for the gentler sex had been designed to be less rough, and were meant to prevent players from over-exercising their delicate natures. But through their skills and successes, the Grads had managed to demonstrate that women and sport activity were not mutually exclusive. As team member Babe Belanger said, the Grads didn't feel their activities and behaviour were any more restricted than that of any other women of similar age. "We had to be clean and neat, our shoes had to be

white and even off the court we had to be well-dressed."
Unladylike habits such as smoking and drinking were
forbidden. The girls were also chaperoned while travelling, and dating was discouraged — although at least
one player managed to meet her husband-to-be on a
road trip. The hard-playing team's good taste and mod-
esty was much admired. Indeed, despite his earlier worries, even Naismith would eventually applaud the
Grads' ability to play basketball while remaining
refined. "My admiration and respect go to you because
you have retained the womanly graces, notwithstanding
your participation in a strenuous game." Challenging
the old beliefs, the Grads became trailblazers for women
in sport in Canada. Next stop, the world.

On June 19, 1924, a headline in the *Edmonton
Journal* read: "Popularity of Grads is shown by send off:
Thousands Congregate at Depot to Say Farewell to City's
Idols." The day before, a band had played "The Maple
Leaf Forever" as the excited crowd watched the equally
excited ladies board a train to eastern Canada. From
Montreal, the Queens of the Court would travel on an
ocean liner to Europe for their first overseas tour.
Having raised the enormous sum of $11,000 to fund
their travel, the Grads thanked all of their supporters,
including their employers, who had generously given
them short leaves from their jobs. What an adventure,

The "Grads" of 1924. Top row (from left to right): Eleanor Mountifield, Connie Smith, J. Percy Page, Abbie Scott, and Daisy Johnson. Bottom row: Nellie Perry, Mary Dunn, Winnie Martin (captain), and Dorothy Johnson.

what an honour to be representing Canada abroad! The team could hardly believe their good fortune. As the girls prepared to depart on their tour, their fans in Edmonton wondered aloud if the team would find worthy opponents at last. The modest team members, of course, would only say, "if we lose to a better team, we will be the first to congratulate them... but we're not thinking of losing!"

The Grads did not lose one game on their European tour, which included exhibition games at the

Olympics. They were proclaimed undisputed world champions. Many fans wondered if the women would retire after their overseas successes, but five years later, in 1929, James Naismith came to Edmonton to see the Grads still playing. Only a few changes to the team had occurred over the years due to marriages and retirements. (Women were generally not permitted to play if they were married; one Grad had to hide her wedding from Mr. Page for a whole month until the season was over.) The newspapers were still full of their one-sided games. Fans, now expecting the team to win, were no longer jamming the arenas, except at the international contests like the Underwood. The greater the likelihood of a Grad defeat, the greater the attendance and gate receipts, which the Grads needed to keep going. Merchants in Edmonton took out ads to show their support, well aware of the enormous publicity and goodwill the team had generated. The Grads had created city loyalty in a place where only one Edmontonian in four had been born there. They helped to rekindle the optimistic pioneering spirit of the west that had been sapped by the Great War and the Great Depression. The players were in constant demand at social functions and public gatherings, where they had as much fun as decorum allowed.

Unlike many American teams who accepted

corporate sponsorship or financial assistance, the Grads continued to be genuine "amateurs," not earning a penny from their playing. They turned down an offer to turn professional in the U.S., where they would have played on theatre stages. Still hoping that women's basketball would one day be an official Olympic sport, the Grads wanted to stay amateur and eligible. By the early 1930s they had travelled more than 200,000 kilometres looking for competition. Their fourth time at the Olympics was at the 1936 Games in Berlin, Germany. And, while women's basketball was still not included officially, the men's game was for the first time.

James Naismith was 75 years old in 1936. He had been asked by the International Olympic Committee to toss up the first ball at this inaugural Olympic tournament, as well as watch the ladies' exhibition matches. Because of their fame, the Grads were invited for the first time to march in the opening ceremonies in Canadian Olympic blazers. The ladies would talk about the pageantry and the precision of the parade for the rest of their lives. Sitting in the athletes' section, they could see Germany's leader, Adolph Hitler. His signs of war preparation were everywhere in Germany, but the country first wanted to show the world its self-proclaimed superiority in the highest arena of sport — the Olympics.

The men's basketball tournament was contested on an outdoor cinder court like the one the Grads had played on their first season. Naismith didn't know who to cheer for at the gold medal game. He was torn between rooting for the country of his birth (Canada) or the country where he had invented the sport (the U.S.). The U.S. team won. In the women's exhibition games played by the Grads, Naismith could see the Grads' style of play hadn't changed, even if some of their faces had. The Canadian women were still clearly superior, and their spirit of cooperation remained unequalled. Once again, Naismith pronounced them the world's best team.

By 1936, the Grads had been playing for over 20 years and would play for five more before ending their dynasty. Their record: 502 wins and only 20 losses over 25 years. Nine times they had played men's teams, and had lost only twice. Naismith wrote to them a few years before his death: "Your record is unparalleled in the history of basketball. My admiration is not only for your record of clean play [but] especially for your unbroken record of good sportsmanship ...You are not only an inspiration to basketball players throughout the world, but a model of all girls' teams. Your attitude and success have been a source of gratification to me in illustrating the possibilities of the game."

The man who had best articulated James Naismith's vision of the game, Percy Page, was also getting older. The Grads' only coach since the team's inception, he hinted that he was ready to retire after the Olympics in Berlin. Page soon turned his considerable influence to politics, and ran successfully as an independent for Alberta's Legislative Assembly.

None of the fiercely loyal players wanted to continue without their "Papa." Page had coached his players from the time they were novices with barely enough strength to toss the ball up against the backboard, to a point where they were all able to sink a perfect one-handed basket on the run. He remained their inspiration until 1940, when the Royal Canadian Air Force took over their arena for drills during World War II.

By that time, there was really nobody left to play anyway. Virtually invincible, the Edmonton Grads were victims of their own success. But they had accomplished their goal: to combine athleticism with the respectable female behaviour of the time. Their success opened gym doors for girls and women keen to follow in their footsteps. And although it did take several decades after the Grads retired, women's basketball was officially added to the Olympic Games in 1976.

Bobbie Rosenfeld
Canada's Superwoman of Sports

"What was I supposed to do — become an invalid?"
Bobbie Rosenfeld

O f all the sports that Fanny "Bobbie" Rosenfeld dared to play before it was acceptable for women to be athletes, her favourite game was ice hockey. Before the 1920s, men monopolized the few indoor arenas that were available, so girls were forced to play hockey on outdoor rinks. Though this meant they often had to play in the biting winds and freezing temperatures of Canadian winters, the young women persevered. During one of their outdoor games, the temperature hit –26 degrees Celsius, but Bobbie and her tomboy friends played on. In fact, they didn't even notice the cold until one of Bobbie's slapshots (she was the only girl who could master the powerful new kind of shot) hit the goalpost and, as Bobbie put it, "shattered in 29,000 pieces!"

In those days, women had to be tough to play hockey but not show it. When Bobbie first started to play for a team, she had to suit up in a modest jersey and a heavy knee-length skirt. This skirt — along with the newspapers stuffed in her long, woollen stockings — helped to protect her from the puck. The restrictive clothing also helped to ensure that Bobbie and the other women didn't play like the roughneck men. They knew that if they did play rough, they would most likely be ridiculed by their families, and would be pressured to quit the unladylike game. Bobbie, for one, didn't want this to happen. Finding a sufficient number of girls for a hockey team was hard enough before the 1920s. Hockey may have been Canada's most popular sport, but in the early part of the 20th century, women like Bobbie were still expected to watch from behind the boards.

Bobbie, though, couldn't and wouldn't stick to just watching. The toughness she developed playing hockey, in spite of the restrictions, helped to prepare her for a life as a pioneer in women's sports. As a child, she had spent many years playing sports with her athletic older brother and his friends. Even though she wasn't big or muscular, she grew up confident and assertive, always pushing herself hard and driving for a goal, a point, or a finish line.

Bobbie didn't only excel at hockey. Softball was a slightly more respectable sport for women in those days, with more than 50 teams in the Toronto area. Bobbie was an outstanding softball player, and because of her impressive talents in this game, her team used to attract more spectators than the local semi-pro men's team. Bobbie also kept busy playing tennis and lacrosse, and she even played basketball against the Edmonton Grads. She was a star in all the sports she played, partly because she was so quick on her feet. In fact, her fast feet on the track led her to the Olympics, where she would leave her greatest mark.

Bobbie's first real race took place at the sideshow of a softball tournament. Her fellow ballplayers encouraged the gregarious and speedy shortstop to run the 100 yard dash, and Bobbie thought, "why not?" Not bothering to change out of her uniform "pup tent" bloomers and stockings for the run, she didn't realize that the city champion, Rosa Grosse, would be running in the same race. As the race began, the cheering crowd of spectators pumped Bobbie up. Once her long legs were in gear on the cinder track, they didn't stop. Spectators always love a close race, and a close race they had that day. The 17-year-old Bobbie came out as the winner, only two-fifths of a second off the women's world record. No one had coached Bobbie in how to run this race. In fact, Bobbie never had a coach in any of her sports since few coaches took female athletes seriously. Playing other sports probably helped Bobbie's conditioning and speed. Her family joked that the only sport she didn't excel in was swimming.

Bobbie's parents had emigrated from Russia in 1905, when she was just an infant. Escaping religious persecution like thousands of others, her Jewish family settled in Barrie, Ontario, where Bobbie spent a very active childhood playing sports. She remembers her father often cheering for her in heavily accented English, "dat's mine goil." At 16, Bobbie earned her nickname when she cut her hair in the "bobbed" style just coming into fashion. By her late teens, she had outgrown all the hometown competition, girls and boys, so she moved to Toronto to search for a job and more challenges. She didn't waste time finding either. In 1924, she won the Toronto tennis championships. The Patterson Chocolate Company hired her as a stenographer and, recognizing her potential, set up a company athletic club called the St. Pats. The next year, the St. Pats club won the Ontario Ladies Track and Field Meet with first place finishes in discus, the 220-yard race, hurdles, and long jump. St. Pats also won second place in javelin and in the 100-yard race. Bobbie was the only member of the club entered in the meet. Incredibly, she had never even competed in discus or javelin before that competition.

Bobbie kept winning trophies and publicity for her company, but she also joined a new club that was just for women, the Toronto Athletic Club. With more women to train and compete with, Bobbie was able to improve her athletic skills. For sportswear, the women had taken to wearing baggy black shorts that looked something like the bloomers ladies had to wear under their long skirts in the 19th century. Bobbie had to tie a rope around her waist so that the "shorts" wouldn't fall down. For one meet, she wore her brother's t-shirt and swim trunks, and used her father's socks in her dark lace-up leather shoes. Even in a big city like Toronto, it was still difficult to find athletic wear for women in the 1920s.

Despite her makeshift athletic attire, Bobbie continued to excel in track and field. During the 1928 National Championships in Halifax, she set Canadian records in broad jump and discus that would not be broken until the 1950s. She also managed to qualify for the Canadian national track team that day. This team would be the first in Canada to participate in track and field events for women at the Olympics in Amsterdam later that year. Two of the other women who qualified for the national team were Ethel Smith and Myrtle Cook, teammates of Bobbie's from the Toronto Athletic Club. But neither of these women was even sure that they could go to the Games. They were both engaged to be married and their wedding dates had been set. When their husbands-to-be permitted postponements, the newspapers commented that both men must have had "the patience of [the Biblical] Job." Perhaps these men were early equalists. After all, it would be another year before the Supreme Court ruled that women were actually "persons."

In 1928, the Olympics had opened track competitions to females on a limited trial basis. Only five track and field events were deemed acceptable for women: the 100 metre, 4 x 100 metre, and 800 metre running races, as well as the discus and high jump contests. "Undignified" events like long jump and standing broad jump were restricted to men. There had been such a controversy about even opening five events to women that the International Olympic Committee (IOC) made its members vote on the experiment. Even the President of the IOC thought the inclusion of women would be "uninteresting" and "wrong," and Canada's delegate to the IOC voted against it, too. In the end, the majority of the members voted in favour of girls competing in the five events, but some countries were still opposed to the idea and did not send females on their teams that year. The more enlightened British team boycotted the track events to protest the fact that women were restricted to only five events when men had 22. In Canada, only six women — and 49 men — were selected to represent the country.

In spite of the restrictions, 23-year-old Bobbie Rosenfeld was thrilled to get the chance for stronger competition and to show the world that women could run, jump, and throw. The Canadian women's track team was dubbed "The Matchless Six" for their record-breaking potential. Besides Bobbie, Myrtle Cook, and Ethel Smith, runners Jane Bell and Jean Thomson, and high jumper Ethel Catherwood made up the team. Only the eldest of the group, 26-year-old team captain Myrtle Cook, had ever been overseas before.

The excited team was sent off by thousands of family and friends, many of whom had raised money for the women's travel through bake sales and donations. Dressed in white pleated flannel skirts, white silk stockings, and red shoes and hats, the women boarded the SS *Albertic* in Montreal, carrying the high hopes of their country. Bobbie and her relay team practiced baton passing every day on the ocean voyage. The team manager insisted the women follow the same training schedule as the men: two workouts a day and a proper diet. When he caught some of them drinking pop, he rebuked them sternly, "You can enjoy yourselves after you have won at Amsterdam." None of this deterred Bobbie from having her usual fun. She kept her teammates relaxed on board with poker games, dancing, and practical jokes. When they arrived in Amsterdam a couple of weeks later, there was no Olympic Village to welcome them. Instead, Bobbie and her teammates bunked together in a rooming house assigned to "Empire" teams. At that time, old world Europe still considered Canada part of the British Empire.

Bobbie, however, would soon demonstrate how independent her adopted Canada had become. After World War I, when Canada had discovered it could do anything as well as any country, nothing seemed out of reach. Bobbie, for one, was itching to test herself against the world's best. Since they were not able to get much practice time in the stadium, the Canadian girls chased streetcars near their rooming house while waiting for the Games to start. During the opening ceremonies, the rain held off for the three-hour march of nations. Never had there been so many women in the parade.

The 100-metre race was the first Olympic event for

the Matchless Six. Minutes before the race, Bobbie was entered as a replacement for Jane Bell, whose old leg injury had flared up. Bobbie easily won her heat and qualified for the finals, as did Myrtle and Ethel. Also qualifying were American athlete Elizabeth "Betty" Robinson and two German competitors. When the finals for the 100-metre were set for the same time as the discus event she was supposed to compete in, Bobbie was forced to withdraw from the discus competition.

Just as the finals were about to begin, Bobbie looked up from her position on the track to the stands. A huge crowd was already cheering and clapping loudly. This was a momentous occasion even for the spectators: girls were running for medals for the first time in the Olympics! Energized by the crowd, Bobbie knew she was more than ready to take on the world. She could hear people in the stands chanting CA-NA-DA, CA-NA-DA! The girls gouged out places in the wet cinder track to give their toes traction for the start — makeshift starting blocks. Bobbie sensed that Myrtle was very tense, and had no luck joking her out of it. To be forerunners of women sprinters everywhere was an honour, but the extra pressure was nerve-racking.

"On your mark" came the first command. Then, "get set." Hands just behind the starting line, arms straight, hips and heels raised, first one woman then another couldn't help but break out too early. Every time the false start was called, the runners had to get set all over again. Each runner was allowed only two false starts before she was disqualified. After yet another false start, a stunned Myrtle Cook and one of the Germans were waved off the track. Myrtle crumpled in a heap and began to cry. Officials gently moved her onto the infield beside the track, where she continued to sob, head buried in her arms, long after the race was over.

Lining back up at the start for the fifth time, Bobbie had to hold back now, slightly unnerved by Myrtle's disqualification. She knew she was still up against the world's best, but Myrtle Cook, who held the Canadian and world record in this event, had been Canada's best hope. It was now up to Bobbie and Ethel.

Bobbie winked at Ethel, digging her toes into the cinder. "Get set…" Bobbie looked straight ahead, her jaw set. She shifted her hips up and moved her body forward until her weight was balanced on her fingertips. "Go!" With the crack of the gun, the four remaining women were off down the track, making history with their feet. Betty Robinson took off the fastest from the blocks, but Bobbie soon surged ahead. Less than 13 seconds later at the finish line, it was difficult to tell who had arrived there first. In those days, there were no photo finishes or instant replays. The German judge was supposed to choose who came first, the French judge who came second. Both judges picked Betty Robinson, so it was up to the remaining American judge to decide who had touched the tape first. He awarded first place to Miss Betty Robinson from the United States with a time of 12.2 seconds. Bobbie was second, and Ethel third. Other witnesses at the finish claimed Betty had touched the tape with her hand, which would have disqualified her. The Canadian team wanted to register a protest and ask that the race be run again. Their team leader, however, wouldn't support such an unsportsmanlike complaint. In any case, the American judge eventually resigned over all the criticism.

Bobbie's reaction to the whole mess was to make light of it. Always the comedian, she joked with her pals that if she had won gold, she would have been given a synagogue back in Toronto, but now all she would get was a pew. Despite all of the conflict after the 100-metre, Canadians had still won two of the first three medals awarded to women in an Olympic race. It was indeed a day to be remembered.

Bobbie couldn't dwell on her near win; she still had other races to run. She did not train or plan to compete in the 800-metre race, but was asked to enter the middle distance to support the youngest member of their team. The race was difficult because runners had to go almost at a sprinter's pace, but for much longer than a sprint usually lasted. Canada's Jean Thompson was a shy, quiet teenager who had unfortunately injured her leg in training the week before the race. She had been restricted to bed, missing critical preparation time. When race day came, Jean decided to try, bandaged leg and all. She looked strong at first, running in the middle of the pack of nine. During most of the race, Bobbie was running in last place. But when she saw Jean get jostled by another runner and falter, Bobbie pumped her arms harder and sprinted up behind Jean. Fifty thousand spectators, including sprinter Percy Williams, who had just won two gold medals for Canada, cheered this incredible effort. Some thought Bobbie could and would pass Jean, but Bobbie knew this was Jean's race. She would not pass her; she just had to urge Jean to keep going. Sprinting for 30 metres at the end of the long race, she pushed Jean into fourth place. Bobbie placed an amazing fifth, but first in sportsmanship.

Along with others, Jean and Bobbie collapsed on the field at the end of the race, both having beaten their personal best times as well as the world record. Olympic officials, especially the ones who had voted against including track events for women, showed concern. This evidence of exhaustion only encouraged their argument that girls were not meant to run so far so fast, even though men also collapsed from exhaustion in the same middle distance races. Although other track and field events continued for women after the 1928 Games, the 800-metre race was closed to women until 1960.

Bobbie was outraged, but as a woman in 1928, she was also well used to the discrimination. Responding to reporters' questions with jokes and sarcasm, she told them she did not have the strength to train more than twice a week for these "long" races. Tongue-in-cheek, she also said she needed two pints of beer daily to keep her energy up. Later, when *Maclean's* magazine asked what Bobbie seriously thought of the debate, she didn't hesitate to speak her mind. "If a girl passes a medical examination and trains properly, she should be capable of this distance." She knew she herself hadn't trained for the longer distance of the 800-metre, but she said "there was no undue effort required to enable me to finish it."

At any rate, Bobbie hardly had any time to "recover" from the 800-metre before having to run in her next race, the 4 x 100 relay. The heavily favoured Canadian relay team, including the recovered Myrtle Cook, had a chance for redemption. But they had one injured team member and one replacement member in Bobbie. These women had never run as a team before. Canada's men's team had just been disqualified for dropping the baton, but both the Canadian and the American women's teams easily made the finals, breaking the women's world record in the process.

On the cold wet final day of the Games, the Canadian women, wrapped in their bright red Hudson's Bay blankets, were easy to spot in the stadium. Underneath the blankets they wore red shorts and white t-shirts decorated with a huge red maple leaf and the letters C-A-N-A-D-A. Myrtle and Ethel had decided to make their t-shirts daringly sleeveless. They hoped it would give them even more speed. Drawing numbers out of a hat for which lane they would run in, the designated lead-off runner, Bobbie, drew the inside lane. Jumping up and down with her good fortune, she hugged her teammates and wished them luck before taking her position.

This time, it was the aggressive and eager Bobbie who threatened the team's disqualification with her false start. If she false-started a second time, it would be all over for the Canadians. They could not disappoint Myrtle again. The crowd finally fell silent, as if it too felt the tension and importance of this race. But there was no second false start. The lead runners from the six competing countries all took off at the same time. Bobbie set a strong pace, but was in second place handing off the baton to Ethel Smith. Still in second, Ethel passed to Jane Bell, who courageously ran the best time

The 1928 Olympic gold medalists in the 4 x 100m relay (from left to right): Jane Bell, Myrtle Cook, Ethel Smith, and Bobbie Rosenfeld.

of her life around the curve despite her injury. Then, a close call: Myrtle had almost left the passing zone, risking disqualification, before she felt Jane put the baton in her palm. In the lead now, anchor Myrtle Cook could take her revenge against Betty Robinson, who was close on her heels as the anchor for the Americans. Myrtle brought the baton in to the finish line with almost a five-metre lead. Smiles, tears, and gasps of relief filled the stands. This time there would be no controversy. The judges could see the finish clearly and acknowledge that the Canadian relay team had won the race with a time of 48 2/5 seconds, breaking the women's world record in the process.

Bobbie and the girls were still bouncing and embracing each other as the cameraman from a Toronto newspaper tried in vain to keep them still for a photo. Canadians had won worldwide recognition for their outstanding performances that day. Bobbie had collected the most individual points of all the competing athletes. With the points she and the rest of the women won in their track and field events, Canada came in fourth overall at the 1928 Olympics. Canadians at home were so proud of their best finish ever that 200,000 fans greeted Bobbie and the women at the train station in Toronto. A parade of 100 cars and floats carried the pioneers of women's track and field through the city. Bobbie loved every minute of it, speaking individually to many of her admirers along the route. Each woman was presented with a silver tea service while the crowd sang the popular song, "See Them Smiling Just Now."

Unfortunately, Bobbie herself was soon going to find it tough to smile for a while. The year after the Olympics, she was stricken with severe arthritis and had to stay in bed for eight months. She had to use crutches for another year. In 1931, she returned to softball, basketball, and hockey. She led her league in home runs and was voted outstanding player in Ontario hockey. "What was I supposed to do," she asked, "become an invalid?" But, despite her brave front, she had to retire permanently from competitive sports at age 30.

The woman who had never been coached became a coach. Even when her arthritis flared up so badly that she could barely walk, Bobbie organized women's sports leagues and events. She led the women's track team to the 1934 British Empire Games (known now as the Commonwealth Games). She also became a sportswriter for the Toronto *Globe and Mail.* As a coach, sports administrator, and journalist, she continued to be a pioneer and outspoken role model for Canadian girls. Her column, "Sports Reel," was refreshing, cynical, and candid. She wrote knowledgeably about all sports and athletes, but especially about women: "The modern girl is a better worker and a happier woman by reason of the healthy pleasure she takes in tennis, lacrosse, swimming, running, jumping, and other sports."

In 1955, Canada's Sports Hall of Fame inducted Bobbie and her teammates from the Amsterdam Olympics as its first members. Bobbie was also voted Canadian Woman Athlete of the Half-Century. This maverick had proven Canadian women could run and jump and break world records with their strength, endurance, and speed. Every year, the Bobbie Rosenfeld trophy is aptly awarded to the top female athlete in Canada.

Herman "Jackrabbit" Smith-Johannsen
Skiing's Great-Grandfather

"Ski every day there is snow"
Herman Smith-Johannsen

A mong Canada's most legendary skiers is Herman Jackrabbit Smith-Johannsen, a remarkable athlete who enjoyed the equivalent of almost two lifetimes. In his first half-century, he helped bring Nordic (cross-country) skiing from its birthplace in Norway to the Laurentian hills of Quebec. In his second half, he saw the sport flourish all over North America.

Like most Norwegian youngsters in 1878, little

Herman Johannsen was on barrel stave skis as soon as he could stand up. Skiing had been an important part of Norway's culture for at least 4000 years, necessary as it was for transportation, hunting, and war. By Herman's time, skiing had also become the country's favourite form of recreation and sport. The term skiing encompassed cross-country skiing, ski jumping, and what Norwegians called slalom — a course built around and over natural obstacles like boulders and trees. Herman spent his teen years skiing with and against other young men in his community, two of whom would later become famous explorers. Roald Amundsen, the first man to reach the South Pole, and Fridtjof Nansen, who crossed Greenland on skis, were Herman's role models for a lifetime of adventure.

Norway seemed to produce its fair share of explorers and adventurers. As Herman himself said, "A Norwegian never leaves Norway because he doesn't like Norway. He leaves because he has a desire to see the rest of the world." Herman in particular always "wanted to know what was on the other side of the hill." By the time he was a young man, he had already lived in and explored Germany, the United States, and Cuba before arriving in Canada at the beginning of the 20th century. His work in Canada took him to northern Quebec and Ontario — the true wilderness country of the Crees and

Ojibways. At that time, Herman was working as a young mechanical engineer, and was supposed to sell heavy machinery to loggers and railroad companies. To get to his customers, he had to take a train as far as it would go. When he reached the end of the line, he did what came naturally: he travelled by ski.

As he skied his way around northern Quebec and Ontario, Herman's Scandinavian looks and sparkling blue eyes weren't the only things that interested the Native peoples in the area. At first, the sight of his skinny "footwear" made his newfound friends laugh. Familiar only with their traditional snowshoes, they found his long skis to be quite bizarre and humorous. But once the small, wiry Norwegian demonstrated the art of gliding on skis, they paid more attention. Later they would make their own skis when he showed them that they could reach their traplines more quickly. The Cree honoured Herman with the title "chief," but they called him *wapoos* (the Cree word for "jackrabbit") for his speed and agility on skis.

By the 1920s, Canada had become Chief Jackrabbit's permanent home. He had discovered no other country better suited to the sport of skiing. Canada's ski season was long and abundant with snow. It also boasted more daylight hours than Scandinavia in the winter. Jackrabbit gravitated to the Laurentian hills because they reminded him most of home and eased his transition from the old world to the new. While exploring the unfamiliar wilderness around the villages of St. Sauveur, Ste. Marguerite, and Ste. Agathe, he cut and marked trails to make it easier for the locals to get around. He showed them that ski trails — like the railroad — could bring people together. As a Norwegian, he had always known there was no better form of transportation than du ski (as he learned to say in Quebec).

Around that time, many Canadians were also showing interest in pursuing skiing as a sport and a form of recreation. In 1928, the Canadian National Railroad responded to this increased interest by offering a special ski train on Sundays. This train brought Montrealers north to the hills of the Laurentians. Skiers could go from train stop to train stop or from village to village, pausing for lunch, some singing, or to enjoy a warm fire at one of the inns. On Sunday evenings, the skiers could hop back on the train and return to the city.

Jackrabbit was delighted with the blossoming interest in his favourite sport. To him, there were really only two seasons: one with snow and one without. "On or before the 15th of November I'll be out on my skis every day!" he would crow with glee. Moderation in all things — except skiing — was his motto. Every morning during ski season, Jackrabbit liked to call out, "Who's for skiing this morning?" Dressed in knickers, long woollen knee socks, and his ever-present knapsack, he shared his trails and experience with many new enthusiasts. He told them, "a practical experience is worth more than any number of lessons, so after you've found your 'ski legs', then come with me on a trip in the bush." Like their mentor, these enthusiasts soon found out that skiing released the stresses of city life.

Jackrabbit would also inspire youngsters to start skiing, jovially carrying a child piggyback or on his shoulders until he or she was ready to keep up. His own children, Alice Jr., Bobby, and Peggy, skied like their father — they were like jackrabbits disappearing over the snow, nimbly dodging in and out of the trees. Jackrabbit's wife Alice, who he'd met while skiing in a Cleveland park, had developed her own peculiar style for steep hills. Nervous about the speed, she would put her ski poles between her legs for brakes, and then ride them down the hills like she was riding a broomstick.

In 1929, the Great Depression struck. Jackrabbit and his family, like countless others, found themselves suddenly penniless. But while others jumped out of windows over collapsed businesses and worthless stocks, Jackrabbit tried to assure his family that they would weather the storm. Even after his home's telephone service, electricity, and heating were cut off, he told them: "Life is like a canoe trip. You have good weather, and you have bad weather, but for those who wait long enough, the sun always comes out again." His antidote for easing business worries had always been skiing, and he soon decided that it would also be the basis for his new career.

In 1931, the Johannsen family moved in with friends, eventually finding a small summer shack near the ski trails in which to start a simpler life. Jackrabbit was to be a trail cutter and ski expert for hire, a "skiing engineer." He would charge up to $10 a day if and when someone could pay. He went hunting and always had a deer or a moose hanging in the woodshed so that the family could live off the land like his Native friends. The family had already sold their car, given up their refrigerator, and even stopped buying the daily newspaper. Jackrabbit joked that they could get all the bad news they wanted on the radio.

Jackrabbit's reputation and determination helped him find work. The Canadian Pacific Railway (CPR) gave him a pass on their trains. They appreciated all the unpaid work he had done to promote the sport of skiing and encourage travel on their trains. Despite the Depression, hotel owners were starting to realize the possibilities of the ski business and began to hire him. He cut and marked a network of ski trails around

Montebello for the CPR's Seigneury Club and also built a championship-calibre ski jump to attract both athletes and spectators. Since there wasn't a good map of the area, he prepared a skier's guidebook and map to the Laurentian trails. He knew the trails very well since he had cut most of them. Jackrabbit was proudest of his Maple Leaf Trail. He'd had to work hard to gain the support of landowners, governments, and volunteers to cut and mark the 128 kilometres between LaBelle and Shawbridge. The trail went up and over the Laurentian's highest peak, Tremblant, prompting skiers to call it "the high route to heaven."

On January 31, 1930, the Johannsens became Canadian citizens officially. Jackrabbit was pleased. In Canada, he claimed, "I can keep my pride in my 'old country' and at the same time be accepted as a true Canadian." He liked to tell other Canadians, "Preserve your country, preserve the native way of life and preserve yourselves." To him, living in Canada meant living in, and loving, the wilderness. "You can build a fire back in the bush and sleep in your sleeping bag in the snow. You don't even need a tent when it's cold enough. Most of the time the air is dry up north and you're cozy with a big fire. You take a snow bath, and you feel like a million dollars. That's the life."

Jackrabbit never stopped promoting the fun and

fitness of skiing. He was a longstanding member of the Montreal ski club, and his friends there claimed it was one of them who gave their most honoured member his nickname. "Remember that time, when after dark we decided to play 'hare and hounds'? The moon was full, the snow was fresh, and I said, Herman, you be the hare. We'll give you a two-minute start. Then all of us 'hounds' will follow your track and try to catch you before you can get back here to the house. You set off at a great pace, down the gully, off through the deep woods. We followed as best we could, in and out among the trees, down and up again, and finally we heard you holler from way up beside the Lone Elm. Then you swooshed back down here to the lake. 'Just look at that Jackrabbit go!' I shouted as we all streamed after you. But we never did catch you, and you sure had the laugh on us when we panted up to the kitchen door. Somehow the name 'Jackrabbit' stuck."

It was this ski club, with Jackrabbit's help, that hosted the first Canadian downhill race in 1931 at Tremblant. At that time, there were no trails down the mountain so most of the race would consist of bush-whacking through the trees. The 22 competitors from Canada and England skied to the foot of Mont Tremblant and climbed it by way of the fire ranger's trail. From the top, it was up to every racer to beat down what he chose as the shortest and fastest route to the bottom. For most of an hour, the mountain echoed with shouts and yells as bodies crashed through the forest and competitors grasped at trees, rode their poles, or jumped down cliffs. Jackrabbit, the forerunner with the stopwatch, timed the winner in at an impressive 15 minutes and two seconds. The rest of the competitors were satisfied to have just survived the event. (Later, the trail would be turned into a perfectly groomed 1.87-kilometre course that could be skied in less than three minutes.)

The next year, Jackrabbit was asked to co-coach the team that would represent Canada at the 1932 Winter Olympic Games in Lake Placid. Olympic ski events at that time were Nordic and jumping — no bushwhacking or downhill races just yet. After training on the 50-kilometre cross-country course Jackrabbit had set in the Laurentians, the team headed to Lake Placid. Two days before the race, Jackrabbit decided that his boys needed exercise. He got them up early to ski the 16 kilometres to Mount March, then had them climb the 5600-foot peak, breaking trail all the way. It was almost dusk when they reached the top of the mountain and the fire-ranger's trail. Then, down the trail they schussed, dodging trees all the way to the bottom. They finished the 60-kilometre day by skiing back to the village in the dark, with Jackrabbit leading most of the way. Who dared to complain? At what the organizers called his "advanced age of 55," Jackrabbit was also invited to be one of the first to test the 18-kilometre Olympic course. His Canadian team did well, but his former countrymen, the Norwegians, still dominated the skiing medals.

Shortly before the 1932 Olympics, the world's very first rope ski tow was built in Shawbridge, Quebec. A young ski jumper by the name of Alex Foster had had the ingenious idea of taking the wheels off a taxi — useless in the wintertime — and using its motor to pull skiers up Big Hill on a rope. Although interested in the concept and helpful as an engineer, Jackrabbit couldn't imagine paying a nickle a lift. He could climb the hill faster than the tow's five kilometres an hour! Less energetic skiers, however, lined up for the thrill of downhill runs without all the effort of climbing up the hill. Calling this new development "yo-yo skiing," Jackrabbit reluctantly helped to install more ski tows in Quebec and Ontario. It didn't fit his vision of skiing, but he hoped it would attract more Canadians to the sport. In the winter of 1935, 31 ski trains carried a total of 10,000 Nordic skiers to the skier's paradise of the Laurentians. And, for the first time, the Olympic Games in 1936 would include downhill racing, the modern kind of slalom that Jackrabbit called "ballet dancing in a fixed groove around flags."

Occasionally, Jackrabbit participated in races, preferring the longer distances and the rugged bushwhacks. He regularly beat others who were half his age or younger. When he did, he consoled them in his puckish sense of humour by telling them he'd had more years to practise. By 1937, though, it was his children's turn to bring glory to the Johannsen name. That year, Jackrabbit's daughter Peggy won the award for best woman skier in Canada and in 1939, his son Bob was named all-round Canadian champion. Bob then left Quebec to represent Canada in international competition, and to attend university in Norway. World War II broke out while he was there, providing an unexpected and terrifying adventure. When Germany occupied Norway, Bob was detained by the Nazis. Eventually, he escaped to neutral Sweden with the help of Norway's famous underground resistance movement. Back in Canada, Jackrabbit didn't hear from his son for three years. In the meantime, he wanted to help with the war effort somehow. He offered to train the ski troops but officials told him he was "much too old." The 65-year-old had skied over 1600 kilometres that year!

Jackrabbit watched in despair as skiers began leaving ski touring in droves for what he now called "the evils of rope tows." By 1941, there were 44 ski tows in Canada and the number grew after the war brought new prosperity to the country. The tireless senior citizen still couldn't understand their appeal. "I've frozen a lot running downhill in cold weather and I'll be darned if I want to freeze going uphill too." Even the ski equipment used for downhill was different, Jackrabbit complained. "Skiing's gotten to be a money-making racket. Nothing but high priced boards, pretty clothes, and lazy people." He had to cut new cross-country runs to avoid the new roads, houses, and ski lifts that were ruining his old runs. In 1950, at 75 years old, Jackrabbit placed a respectable third in a race against many youngsters, but then decided that was enough racing. "My wife has to stay up at night massaging my cramping legs." He had never taken any pills, and he didn't plan on starting.

In his 86th winter, Jackrabbit bumped into Canada's top downhill ski racer, Nancy Greene, at the bottom of Mont Tremblant's chairlift. He congratulated her on winning her alpine race that day but told her a real skier would not wait in lift lines. "I'll beat you to the top," he teased. Sure enough, when Nancy reached the top of the mountain via the chairlift, Jackrabbit was already there, not even out of breath after skiing to the top on his cross-country skis. She was duly impressed.

In 1963, Jackrabbit's wife Alice died. He had always called her "the most wonderful good luck in his life." She was 81 when she passed away, and for 56 years she had kept the home fires burning. Her rocking chair beside the hearth was now strangely empty. "Seems I now have to learn the art of living alone," Jackrabbit remarked in his usual stoic Norwegian way. "But I'm used to looking after myself."

Approaching his 100th birthday, Jackrabbit settled into a simple routine: up and dressed by 6:00 a.m., eating porridge by 7:00. After breakfast, attack the woodpile to chop enough logs for the fire and shovel the path. By 8:30, strap on skis and go for the mail. Take the long way, three kilometres, to stop and chat with neighbours on that route. Back at home, stoke the fire and settle down to the mail — plenty of it from friends and admirers all over the world. By eleven, start to cook lunch — usually some potatoes, onions, and carrots — all in one pot. By noon, lie down for half an hour. By one, go out for a run on skis, but home for the day by four to read by the fire in his moccasins, or chat with visitors. Eat a supper of pea soup or meatballs, flatbread, and goat cheese, maybe listen to the news, but in bed by nine o'clock. On Saturdays, daughter Peggy usually drove up to help with laundry and groceries, to reminisce, and to plan the next adventure. Skiing was his health insurance: he had his sights set on reaching 100.

But Canada's 100th birthday came first in 1967, and that year, Jackrabbit helped establish the first Canadian

Ski Marathon: 160 kilometres from Lachute, Quebec, to Ottawa over two days. In 1972, at 97, he received the Medal of St. Olaf from the King of Norway for his great contribution to the advancement of ski touring in Canada. "Well, for goodness sake," was his surprised response. In Canada, it had taken cross-country skiing 40 years to recover from "tow fever." The hills had finally become as crowded as the city and, as Jackrabbit had predicted, people came back to tour again in the wide-open spaces. He cut new trails and thousands of skiers young and old reappeared. "There are sports that you can [only] play when you're young but you can ski all your life."

Just before his own 100th birthday, Jackrabbit was made a member of the Order of Canada by his skiing friend, Roland Michener. The award was meant to honour lifetime achievement, but Jackrabbit was not ready for his life to be over. "I'm still a young fellow, there's no need for me to pack up yet, I still have many more miles to cover." However, the last time he skied with Roland on the final stretch of the Marathon, he fell and broke his back. Jackrabbit could still kid, "When a governor general beats you, it's time to quit ski racing."

When asked what it was like to be 100, the ever-practical Norwegian answered: "I just have a little trouble with my balance. Have to be careful about falling down as it's getting much harder to get up." He tolerated the huge fuss that was made over his centennial: the parties and the honorary degrees, as well as the films, songs, poems, and book written about him. But afterwards, he commented with a twinkle in his eye, "All my friends have done their very best to kill me off with kindness and good will, but I managed to fool them all. You can bet I'll still be around for another ten years yet!"

A few years later, his Native friends hosted a big party for the North American Cross Country Ski Championships and dedicated it to Jackrabbit. They presented him with a magnificent feather war bonnet as honorary chief. In 1982, he wore bib number 107 to commemorate his age as he skied onto the field at Mooney's Bay in Ottawa. He saluted the cheers with a wave of his ski pole. The national ski body had named its Jackrabbit Ski League program after him a few years earlier and asked him to present the medals for the Jackrabbit ski day. He joked with the young skiers, "I'm steadier on skis with two poles to hold me up. But I'm not as good a skier as I was 100 years ago." Jackrabbit did feel he had achieved his two goals: he had witnessed cross-country skiing regain its popularity and he had skied for more than 100 years. He told the young skiers to ski everyday there was snow and maybe they'd ski for more than 100 years, too.

In 1986, the world's oldest athlete, Jackrabbit Johannsen, finally passed on. He had lived life to its fullest for more than 111 years. His family buried him and then went for a moonlight ski. In the Laurentians, Jackrabbit's cozy little Norwegian mountain hytte, a place for contemplation, served as a ski museum honouring his achievements. There, a visitor could almost hear Jackrabbit still saying, "Climb your mountain slowly, one step at a time and when you stand upon the summit, look further, beyond the farthest horizon." Nearby on Mount Tremblant, Johannsen Peak offers an amazing view.

Father David Bauer
Canada's Hockey Crusader

"Make use of technique, but let the Spirit prevail."
Father David Bauer

F ather David Bauer grew increasingly dismayed as he watched Canada battle Sweden for the 1962 World Hockey Championships. Even from his seat high up in the Colorado Springs arena, he could sense the Canadian players' frustrations. A referee had just sent yet another Canadian player to the penalty box for unnecessary roughness. To lose the game would be bad enough, but to lose it through penalties would be disgraceful.

Surveying the action on the ice below, Father Dave believed that the Canadian team (the Galt Terriers) was outclassed. The top-level amateur teams in Canada were simply too accustomed to playing old-style hockey. For the last 10 years, Father Dave had been seeing this old style challenged by the new, swift skating and stick-handling European style. The Russian and Czechoslovakian teams in particular had been carefully studying the Canadian game of hockey. They'd learned to play it with strategy and grace, but without the classic Canadian roughness. In the 1956 Olympics, the Russians had defeated Canada's national team, the Kitchener-Waterloo Dutchmen, which had been coached by Father Dave's brother.

The Russian and Czech national teams had not made it to the 1962 tournament, however, and Canadian hockey fans had expected an easy gold medal. But Father Dave could see that the days when his nation dominated world hockey tournaments were truly gone. Even Sweden was beating Canada at this tournament! It had been 10 long years since the Edmonton Mercury team had won Canada's last gold medal in Olympic hockey. Before that, Canadian teams hadn't known how to lose. Canada, after all, had invented the game. Now, the 1962 Galt Terriers would have to slink back home and face the disgust of hockey fans across the nation. As they and Father Dave well knew, hockey was not just a game to Canadians.

With Canada's image in international hockey dying, the country needed a miracle. Because International and Olympic hockey rules only allowed amateurs to play, Canada had usually been represented by a Senior A club team — either the most recent winner of the Allan Cup or a city team whose players could afford to take time off work and pay their own way. Other countries without professional leagues like the National Hockey League (NHL) had different interpretations of "amateur." Russian players, for example, were given government "jobs" but were never asked to do anything except play hockey year-round. Their housing, food, travel, equipment, and perks were all provided. Meanwhile, Canadian Senior A teams still had to pass the hat at their home games to cover expenses. How could Canada's part-time amateur teams compete with this system sarcastically dubbed "shamateurism"?

Father Dave had an idea. Once a formidable hockey player himself, he now coached the top level of amateurs. He had won the Memorial Cup (Canada's junior championships) in 1943 as a left-winger, and again in 1961 as a coach. These successes allowed him to make a bold proposal to the Canadian Amateur Hockey Association (CAHA) in 1962. That year, he told the CAHA board of directors that Canada needed a national team. Not just a city team that happened to win the national championships, but an all-star team, selected from the country's best amateur hockey players.

When he was growing up in Waterloo, Ontario, David Bauer, like the majority of Canadian boys, had wanted to do nothing more than play hockey. He was the youngest boy of 11 children, and his sisters used to have to physically drag him off the frozen ponds to get him to school. One of his older brothers played professional hockey and David was determined to follow his lead. But at 16, when he took off for an NHL Boston Bruins training camp without permission, his father, Edgar, threatened to take the next train out and chase after him. As David would later remember, "It was then that my father told me that I would be a professional hockey player before I got an education over his dead body." After the lecture, Edgar coaxed the disappointed boy home. A compromise was soon reached by enrolling David at St. Michael's College in Toronto. The unusual school combined high school classes with the most competitive junior hockey program at the time, and David excelled at both.

Upon his graduation from St. Mike's, David discovered that his options for the future were stark: he could go to university *or* he could play hockey. (University hockey wasn't top calibre then.) Perhaps anticipating his opportunity to lead by example, he wrestled with his decision for only a short while. He packed up his skates to become a Roman Catholic priest and a teacher with the Basilian congregation. He was later assigned to his alma mater, St. Michael's College, where he could combine teaching with coaching hockey.

In 1962, after having watched the Canadian team swing sticks at Sweden during the World Championships, Father Dave knew something had to done about the rough, old-style hockey the Canadians played. Along with his suggestion to the CAHA that Canada have an all-star national team came another revolutionary idea. He proposed that the national team players have the option to attend university. Father Dave wanted young men to have the chance his generation hadn't had: to play hockey *and* go to school. He knew that many top amateur players were recruited for NHL farm teams before they even finished high school. Unfortunately, only very few of these players actually made it out of those leagues into the NHL, and when their time in hockey ended, they were left without a high school diploma or another career. Father Dave reminded the CAHA, "The whole point of amateur sport should be the welfare of the participants. Amateur sport should not be a business." This, of course, was not a popular notion at a time when playing for the NHL was the epitome of most young male Canadians' dreams.

The CAHA agreed to give Father Dave the chance to experiment with this revolutionary idea, and he was soon criss-crossing Canada to gather disciples for his crusade. He told potential recruits, "It is an honour to represent Canada. You know too, that you will undoubtedly improve as hockey players. You are doing what you can to reconstruct amateur hockey in Canada. Somebody has to show school and hockey can be combined to make things easier for the kids that will follow you."

Father Dave was persuasive but also selective. He demanded disciplined hockey players — superstars and goons need not apply. He wanted only agile, fast, team players who could keep up with the remarkable European skaters on the larger ice surface. Many recruits came from his alma mater, St. Mike's, and these players already knew a little about what it was like to combine school and hockey. Other recruits were on their way to university, thinking they had to give up hockey. Father Dave's most skilled recruits were, of course, the same players that the professional leagues wanted. The pros tempted the young men with starting salaries of $8000 to $10,000 plus bonuses and the chance to be an NHL star someday. Father Dave could only offer room, board, and tuition. But the gentle, charismatic priest swayed many with his idealism and his passion for the game. The 1960s was the decade to challenge the status quo. One recruit explained that he wanted "a purpose for playing hockey beyond the making of money for one's self and the team owners." The cream of Canada's hockey youth had a chance to make a difference in the game they and Father Dave loved. Many of them signed on to be a part of his team.

Father Dave's crusade would still have its crosses to bear. In 1963, he was teaching at the Basilian college of St. Mark's at the University of British Columbia. His Basilian community supported the educational value of sport in theory, but his fellow priests were sometimes sceptical. The violent reputation of hockey did not fit with a religious life. Father Dave's mission was formidable: to change hockey's image through building this different kind of team. The university had agreed to provide the players' education, but that was all. At first, the team didn't even have a rink to play on. There were only two rinks in Vancouver at the time, one for the professional team and one for everyone else. Father Dave managed to wheedle three practice times a week — two at night and one at noon. He would have liked to practise more, but he knew university courses demanded the players' attention, too. This left the team with barely six months to practise and play together before their first major competition. Could they make themselves into a better team than the Senior A teams that had been representing Canada to date?

Father Dave wasn't sure. "It was a giant act of faith. It was crazy...we had no uniforms, no ice, no schedule, no base, no money. Nothing!" But he tirelessly solicited support, convincing family friends and even his own mother to help out with a few thousand dollars. The team members became resourceful, too. Claiming an abandoned wreck of a building on campus, they renovated it into a makeshift dorm. One bathroom served 18 players in the hectic mornings before classes. In the evenings, study sessions and wild card games held at the dorm helped the players gel as a team. Father Dave also hired an elderly den mother to cook inexpensively for the hungry athletes. They quickly learned that if they complimented an entree too liberally, they would be served the same thing for the next five days. Once, when the team was running out of money for food, Father Dave invited a reporter to see their Spartan living conditions. The reporter's article prompted other believers, including the federal government, to invest in Father Dave's dream.

The group of Canadian hockey players now had food, beds, and ice time, but they still needed competition to help them prepare for their goal: the 1964 Olympics. Whom could they play against? The national team experiment was a new standard and calibre of play. They would have liked to test themselves against the pros, but the NHL was uncooperative. Its president, Clarence Campbell, accused Father Dave of being "a hockey man, who just moonlights in the priesthood, unfairly competing for their players." Father Dave's inspirational leadership was indeed tough competition. His players developed a strong loyalty to him and to his vision.

In January of 1964, the new experimental team, later known as the "Nats," packed their equipment for a pre-Olympic exhibition tour. They may have been under-prepared for high-calibre international hockey, but they were keen to display their new style of play. Father Dave had drilled them in a few simple techniques. His favourite lesson was "the best offence is a good defence." Mostly, he expected the players to work hard as a team and play fairly and under control. In the dressing room before games, while the players were lacing up their skates, Father Dave would deliver his sermon: "Part of representing Canada internationally is to provide a good image of this nation. You can play clean, skillful, yet aggressive hockey." A few of the older players rolled their eyes; they weren't yet all believers in this radical idea, but were willing to try it out for Father Dave's sake. "You can forget all about the tactics that your other coaches may have encouraged you to use to win. We do not need to take penalties." All the players nodded in agreement; they knew the Russians were famous for their dangerous power play. "We will play to win, but not at any price. Canada has been seen to be ruffians in the past and we want to change that tarnished image. If we cannot, we will have not accomplished anything worthwhile, even if we do win." Tell that to the fans, some players thought to themselves.

During the pre-Olympic tour, the Nats' opponents were the ones playing rough this time, intent on annoying the Canadian team and pushing them to retaliate. Other teams would hook, slash, spear, and spit on the Nats. At first, the Canadian players turned the other cheek. Father Dave's Nats would do almost anything for their coach but their resolve was being severely tested. After one game in the series, the teammates held a secret meeting — without Father Dave — to consider dropping out of the tour. Some of the players were worried that they couldn't continue to play without retaliating. They knew quitting would sabotage Father Dave's dream and reflect poorly on him [as a priest]. He had put his reputation on the line for the team. Even without him in the room, Father Dave's presence and message was overpowering. The teammates could almost hear his gentle but firm reminders that they were ambassadors for Canada so had to play with discipline and courage. At the end of the meeting, the team voted to continue Father Dave's crusade.

Showing up at the Olympic Village in Innsbruck, Austria, they were pleased to find that their accommodations were slightly better than what they'd had at the University of British Columbia. Even the straw-filled mattresses and the rowdy South African team upstairs didn't bother the Nats too much. The day before their first game in the Olympic tournament, the team climbed a mountain in Igls to watch the bobsled race. At the top of the mountain, they cheered on the underdog Canadian bobsledders, piloted by Vic Emery, and watched them win Olympic gold medals. After that, the team didn't need pep talks from Father Dave or anyone else. In the opening game of their hockey tournament, the inspired Nats played their hearts out for the Canadian flag. They beat Switzerland 8-0. The European spectators were amazed to see Canadian players who didn't fight or scream at the officials, even when they had good reason to do so. It was hard not to credit the man behind the bench, Father Dave, who, wearing his fedora and clerical collar, watched his team with pride.

Canada's match against Sweden didn't go quite as smoothly. During that game, a Swedish player accidentally broke his stick and threw it at the Canadian bench nearby. He then skated to his own bench to get a new one, unaware of the bedlam behind him. The stick had hit Father Dave in the face and cut his forehead. Blood gushing from his wound, Father Dave hardly had the chance to wipe it off before he had to grab some of his players by the backs of their jerseys. He restrained them from jumping over the boards to retaliate on his behalf. Appealing to the self-discipline he had nurtured, he called for calm. The trainer tried to bandage Father Dave up, but the priest was too busy attempting to control his flock. The spectators were also howling at the Swede's bench, and at the referee. Incredibly, no penalty was called, and the priest insisted to his players that the game must go on. This was the Nat's most crucial test so far. Father Dave kept several of the still-furious players on the bench in the last minutes of the game. He didn't want anyone tempted by revenge. The Nats were winning the game and winning it cleanly.

A huge outcry followed the game, but it was not led by the Canadians. The Swedish player was suspended for one game. The referee of the game was also suspended for not giving the penalty right away. No one on the Nats team was surprised when Father Dave accepted an apology and invited the suspended player to watch the Czech vs. USSR game with him the next evening. The fans and hockey fraternity, however, were amazed. They cheered all the Canadians, especially Father Dave, for this example of true sportsmanship.

Several games later, Canada had still not lost a game in the tournament. Only the two toughest opponents — Russia and Czechoslovakia — were left to play. The Nats were to face these teams in games scheduled not even 24 hours apart.

In the third period of their match-up with the Czechs, the Nats were leading 1-0. But seven minutes before the end of the game, the Nat's unbeatable goalie suffered an injury when a Czech player skated into his crease. Seth Martin had to leave the game for the last critical minutes. The game turned as the Czechs made three quick goals to win.

Before Canada's final game against the unbeaten Russian team, Father Dave visited the dressing room. As he spoke, the players quietly pulled on their maple leaf uniforms and tightened their skates. He did not have to tell them that the Olympic gold medal was at stake. He cracked a few jokes to break the tension then said, "If you play your best, you can leave the results up to Providence." The pressure was off.

For the first two periods of the final game, the Nats played the same first-rate hockey for Father Dave that they had the whole tournament. The best offence *was* a good defence. The score crept up very slowly, and the

Canadians were in the lead twice. (1-0, 1-1, 2-1.) A full house of 11,000 European hockey fans cheered the Canadian goals. Then the Nats received a rare penalty for elbowing and the Russian power play tied the score at two goals apiece. The Russians scored the only goal in the third period to beat Canada 3-2.

Despite their despair over missing their chance to reclaim Canada's hockey honour, the players tried to sing, "For he's a jolly good fellow'" when Father Dave joined them in the dressing room after the game. They knew they wouldn't have been so close to winning without him. The singing sounded more like crying to the priest. He too was disappointed, but not discouraged. They had lost the gold medal by only one goal, he reminded them. And there was no shame in the way they had played.

At the conclusion of the Olympic tournament, Canada still had the best record of the three teams tied for second so the Nats were told to come to the award ceremonies. They managed to put away their disappointment and get excited about receiving their medals. But during the team's bus ride down to the ceremonies, the Olympic Committee reversed itself. It ruled that the team having scored the most goals against all opposition teams — not just the top four — was the winner. On that basis, Sweden took the silver, and Czechoslovakia beat out Canada for the bronze medal. The whole team was crushed. Some couldn't resist showing it and dumped their fourth place diplomas of participation in the trashcans.

But the dark cloud over the Nats' Olympic experience did have a gold — not silver — lining. Canada did receive a gold medal for hockey at the Games, but not for winning the tournament. Father Dave was presented with a special medal in recognition of his sportsmanship, and for practicing what he preached. (One of his players couldn't help but tease him: "you get a gold medal for a little cut ... I get deeper cuts than that shaving!") The unexpected medal was an immense triumph for Canada's new hockey image. When another of his players later suggested to him, "Father, your flock was fleeced," Father Dave responded emphatically, insisting "this truly amateur team represented Canada with class, dignity, enthusiasm, dedication, and outstanding willingness to compete." The Nats had, in fact, almost pulled off the impossible; with no real international experience and a team of university students just starting to gel, they had almost won Olympic gold by playing good, clean hockey. Father Dave knew the team could only get better. The CAHA considered the experiment a success and wondered if the priest and the team would be willing to continue. Father Dave again appealed to his players: "A lot of people have supported this team. It represents our hopes for rebuilding amateur hockey in Canada. We've put a great deal into it and can't let it die now." And, he added pointedly, "Because Canada might not win at the Olympics is no reason not to proceed again."

Although he couldn't hold all the team members together, eight members of his national team experiment continued in Winnipeg at the University of Manitoba to prepare for the next Olympics. The National Team did win a medal in 1968, but after that, Canada decided to retire from international hockey competition for a while. Even the tough Canadian fans were starting to realize what the Nats were up against in international hockey. Canada eventually convinced the International Ice Hockey Federation to make the competition fairer and more realistic. If other countries could use their professional players, why couldn't Canada? It would take 50 years, but Canada would win back its pride with hockey gold in open (not amateur) competition at the Olympics in 2002.

Father Dave's other prayers were answered, too. A big part of his dream was to see Nats players fulfill their potential in careers outside of hockey. Thirty-one Nats graduated from university and more than twice that number earned valuable degree credits while playing hockey. Pioneers in the hockey world, some became professionals in their various fields of teaching, medicine, and law. Some became successful professional hockey players. A few, like famous NHL goalie and lawyer Ken Dryden, were able to become both.

Hockey has always had a unique position within Canadian culture. As a hockey-coaching priest, Father Dave had wanted to create a better world in hockey. His Nats had a unique opportunity to inspire Canadian hockey youth with dreams beyond the NHL. Against all odds abroad, the team represented Canada with dignity and courage under Father David Bauer's inspiring leadership.

Nancy Greene
The Tiger of
the Slopes

"If you're afraid of falling, you're doomed."
Nancy Greene

P oised on top of Red Mountain, staring down a racecourse that seemed to drop off the side of a cliff, 14-year-old Nancy Greene suddenly recalled that she had never intended to be a ski racer. What she had really wanted to do was skate. But figure skating had turned out to be boringly slow and there was no hockey for girls in her ski-crazy town. Her big sister Elizabeth was a ski racer, and the real reason Nancy was on top of Red Mountain this day. Nancy was determined to beat Liz.

Located deep in the rugged interior of British

Columbia, where Scandinavian settlers had spread their love for skiing, Red Mountain was the peak that Nancy's engineer father had helped tame with a primitive ski lift in 1946. Before the chairlift, the very first in Western Canada, Nancy's family and the other keen skiers in the mining town of Rossland had to herringbone up the slopes for an hour. It only took them a few minutes to ski down. Like her sister, Nancy had learned to ski on homemade skis when she was just a toddler. But Liz was considered the ski racer in the Greene family, a prodigy who won all her races.

At one of these races, the 1958 Canadian Junior Championships held in Rossland, Liz was expected to lead her BC provincial team to victory. But the famously steep hills of Red Mountain were treacherously icy that week. Two of Liz's teammates suffered injuries in the training races and the coach needed spares. Although she wasn't a ranked racer like Liz, Nancy knew the mountain well; it was literally in her backyard. Nancy wasn't scared of ice — or anything else for that matter — and, as Liz knew intimately, she was extraordinarily competitive. The coach called Nancy at home on the eve of the championships and asked if she would be willing to race. True to her nature, Nancy said "Why not?"

The next day, Nancy watched as the two forerunners who were sent down to test the slalom course suffered nasty falls. Both girls skidded on the slick ice and tumbled head over skis the rest of the way down the hill. When it was Nancy's turn to run the course, she was shaking just a little in her lace-up leather ski boots, but she didn't fall. When she reached the bottom, she was relieved that she hadn't embarrassed herself. Shivering on the slow lift heading back up the hill for her second run, she heard her time announced. It sure didn't sound fast. Figuring she was out of the running anyway, she decided it didn't matter what she did on the next run. She would ski like she always skied, for the fun of it. Nancy tucked the tip of her woollen ski hat under her goggles strap and pushed off on her second run, tackling the mountain in her typical daredevil skiing style. Crash! Down Nancy slid, scraping the ice with her thighs, grateful for the extra pair of long underwear and thick baggy ski pants she had put on that morning. Fighting to regain her balance, she quickly got up and kept going. In those days, it wasn't unusual to fall and still be able to place; Nancy went down again another time before finally swooshing across the finish line.

Though she had fallen twice, Nancy shrugged off the disappointment she felt over her second run. After all, what could she expect on her first serious race? As it turned out, the course had been difficult for everyone that day. With her combined times in the two runs,

Nancy — the inexperienced substitute racer — came in third. She surprised everyone in her debut, but sister Liz still came in first.

The downhill race was the next day. Now confident in her abilities, and even more motivated to beat her sister, Nancy kept her wooden skis under control on the downhill course, this time opting to ski with a little more care and a little less speed. She placed second in the downhill, right behind Liz. From then on, there was no turning back. Ski racing had captured Nancy's heart.

Nancy went back to her high school classes, but skied every chance she got. She joined Liz and the Red Mountain Ski Club in their daily training. Each night, the girls' father would quiz them both. How many runs had they made that day? How did their times measure up? And most importantly, how hard had they worked? Nancy's dad hadn't been concerned when Nancy had shown little interest in racing, but now that she had, he wanted to ensure that she took it very seriously — like Liz. Ski racing was far too hazardous to take lightly. Nancy and Liz's mother also knew a bit about what it took to be successful. Long before her girls were born, Helen had been a ski racer as well, and one year made it to the Canadian championships.

The next Canadian Junior Championships were held in Ontario in 1959. That year, Nancy took her first trip on a plane and her first ride on the subway Toronto had just built. Because the Olympics were only a year away, Canada's national coach would be at the 1959 races, scouting talent. Following the championships, Liz and Nancy were both chosen for the Olympic Team try-outs, which were held the following December in Rossland and nearby Kimberley, British Columbia. Liz was selected for the Olympic team immediately after the tryouts, but Nancy still had to prove herself by placing in a few more races. Fortunately, the pre-Olympic competitions were being held near Rossland, in Utah and Colorado. At these competitions, Nancy worked on her personal style, skiing all-out and risking crashes. When she did crash, it was often a spectacular sight for the spectators, but Nancy rarely hurt herself badly. She was still the kid who dared to climb higher in a tree or speed faster down a hill than anybody else. The more she raced, the more she wanted to win. She was learning every day how to use her intelligence, not just her natural determination, to race. "I discovered the fine line in competitive skiing: you must go fast, but you must not go so fast that you lose control of your skis."

Nancy's results and potential impressed the officials so much that she was told at the last moment she would be able to go to the 1960 Olympics at Squaw Valley in northern California. No one expected Nancy to do well at these Olympics, but they thought the experience might help to make her a medal contender in future Games.

At the 1960 Games, young Nancy was dazzled by the way the Olympic athletes were treated. "The recreation huts are really neat ... a free jukebox, and all the free milkshakes you want," she wrote to her mother. Used to racing in her sister's hand-me-downs, she was delighted with all the free ski clothing and equipment the athletes were given as members of the Olympic team. Nancy smiled her way through the weeks of the Games, soaking up the friendly international atmosphere and seeking autographs for her souvenir book. She also managed to fit in some skiing.

Though a blizzard almost ruined the opening ceremonies of the Games, the snow was good news for the skiers, who were dependant on the weather for their events. When asked at the top of her first downhill run in Squaw Valley whether she was nervous, 16-year-old Nancy replied, "Heck no. Why should I be nervous? No one ever heard of me." She placed 26th in the giant slalom, and 21st in the downhill, which turned out to be the second-highest finisher among the Canadians. Best of all, she had finally beaten her sister!

In the Olympic Village, Nancy was thrilled to be rooming with her hero, fellow Canadian Anne

Heggtveit. (Nancy's dad liked to tell her the story of how the Greene and Heggtveit families had met on a cross-country trail near Ottawa. At that time, both Liz and Anne had been too young to ski, so both were riding on their fathers' backs. The next time these girls would meet would be at the Olympics.) As Nancy watched Anne win a gold medal in the slalom race, she realized how much she wanted a gold medal of her own. Nancy — who had finished last in the slalom race — also realized how much she still had to learn, but suddenly she was determined to do whatever it took.

The lessons Nancy still had to absorb were not just about competition, but also about the realities of an expensive and dangerous sport. While Liz opted for university after the 1960 Games, Nancy decided to find a way to finance her travelling with the national team. In those days, all the serious ski racing took place in Europe. Since Nancy's family couldn't afford to send her overseas, and Canada did not yet fund national teams, she and volunteers from her ski club knocked on doors in Rossland to ask for support. Within two weeks, the determined small-town girl was able to leave for the glamorous Alps. She discovered that ski racing was enormously important in many European countries — unlike in Canada at the time — and had a huge, knowledgeable following. Nancy was eager to learn from the acknowledged skiing queens of France and Austria, competing with them in their own backyard. Travelling constantly from one ski race to another, one country to the next, Nancy never stopped gawking at the sights. (In one year, she and the rest of the national team travelled 3200 kilometres in a rickety Volkswagen bus to race in 11 meets over 21 days.)

Late in the season, perhaps a little fatigued from all the travelling, Nancy skied a careless training run and broke her leg. The break gave her unwanted recuperation time at home during the spring skiing season. Nancy knew she would go crazy if she didn't have something physical to do besides studying for her high school finals. In a time when working out was not yet very scientific, she learned how to lift weights to strengthen her leg and the rest of her body.

Coming back from her injury, she was stronger than ever and placed fifth in the World Championship in 1962. Nancy was accustomed to the tougher competition in Europe, and she and everyone else took for granted that she would win the Canadian Championships in Kimberley later in the season. Ironically, it was Nancy's turn to be humbled by a younger sister. That year, 16-year-old Judy Greene came in first at the Canadian Championships. Nancy placed fifth. The stinging blow to her ego, even after she discovered one of her skis had bent, made Nancy realize how she had to be more serious about her equipment preparation. Much later, ski team technicians would take care of all the equipment. When Nancy was racing, she spent hours every evening checking the tools of her trade, filing and sharpening her edges and waxing her own skis.

Nancy couldn't afford to race in Europe the next year. She also disagreed with Canada's practice of sending racers who may not have been as qualified but were able to pay their own way. She and a renegade group of male ski racers stayed home and trained together in Canada's Alps. The Selkirks and the Monashees were just as good as the Alps and had better snow conditions. Nancy was starting to form strong opinions that would be useful later, when she would be asked how to improve Canada's sports system.

Her second Olympics, the 1964 Games in Innsbruck, Austria, were a different story from the first. This time, as a veteran of the ski tour and Canada's top medal contender, Nancy went into the Games perhaps a little too optimistic and overconfident. She also found herself distracted and disappointed by the growing commercialization of the "amateur" games. Although it was technically against the rules, some of her star competitors were being sponsored by ski manufacturers and paid a type of allowance by their countries. It all seemed very unfair to Nancy, and not in keeping with the spirit of the Olympics.

On top of this, the self-described "Queen of Falls" sprained her ankle in a training run and missed five critical days of practice. Disappointed and humiliated, Nancy didn't come close to meeting her or Canada's expectations at the Innsbruck Games, but she vowed not to give up. She could not retire on a losing note. The bad times continued for a while, and Nancy had another spectacular fall in the downhill at the 1966 World Championships in Portillo, Chile. Moving at 40 kilometres per hour, she caught an edge and cartwheeled into an ice wall lining the course. Luckily, she bounced back from relatively minor injuries and raced the giant slalom the next day. All she said was, "if you're afraid of falling, you're doomed." The next season, the team would try out better equipment, including fibreglass skis, plastic boots, and new team helmets. Nancy's helmet sported a tiger on the back, hence her nickname.

Despite her uneven results, Nancy's friendly, bubbly personality made her popular with the media and the ski fans. She usually indulged the public's perception that she was a sweetly wholesome sports heroine, but some days it was harder than others. One time, she caught a bad cold and was so desperate to go back to her room that she deliberately signed a junior team member's name when asked for an autograph by a mob after her race. Only when the fans had been persuaded that she wasn't "our Nancy" did they leave her alone. Nancy's aggressive skiing was also attracting attention from the Old Guard of Alp skiers. They hadn't even realized there were mountains in Canada to practice on!

The whole world of international ski racing was starting to change. In 1967, the World Cup circuit was born. The World Cup intended to add an annual competitive focal point to make skiing more interesting to racers and fans (and sponsors). Skiers would have to be more consistent, winning every other weekend instead of every four years at the Olympics to be true World Champions.

Nancy didn't know how fast the concept would catch on, but she started off the 1967 World Cup season strongly, winning five races. Despite missing three races in Europe because she had to go home for an important (but not a World Cup) meet in Canada, she had enough World Cup points to put her in a close race for the title. She was in third place by the time the last meet of the season rolled around.

This final meet was held in Jackson Hole, Wyoming. The terrain felt very familiar to Nancy — the towering mountains and wide-open spaces reminded her of the

Canadian Rockies. To emphasize the World Cup show-down atmosphere, the racers were outfitted with cow-boy hats and invited to participate in a rodeo. A relaxed Nancy then went on to win the first two giant slalom races handily, even after going through one gate back-wards! On the eve of the last race, Nancy was in the hotel as usual, clowning around with the other racers and try-ing to sharpen her skis. She hadn't felt nervous until someone reminded her, "tomorrow, you can win the World Cup." All she had to do, of course, was win the last race. What a crowning of her career! What a boost that would be to Canada's place in the skiing world!

Suddenly, Nancy could no longer concentrate. Although in eight years she had never once failed to do her own sharpening, she had to leave her skis with one of the other racers. None of her roommates could settle down that night either, so they ended up talking into the wee hours of the morning. When the alarm went off a few hours later, Nancy could hardly stand up she was so dizzy from fatigue. She persevered through her normal routine: 50 sit-ups, 25 push-ups, and 50 squats. After forcing herself to eat her usual good breakfast, she was soon dragging her tired body up the racecourse, trying to memorize its layout. She knew how important it was to remember the exact position of each gate, the angles at which the gates were set, and where each bump and patch of ice or soft snow was on every part of the route. When it was time to run the course, Nancy wasn't supposed to have to think anymore, just do what she had planned in this pre-race preparation.

Waiting at the starting gate in misty falling snow, wearing number 13 on her race bib, Nancy tried to tell herself all she had to do was ski her best. The countdown began and she made a last adjustment to her new plastic boots and dug in her poles. 5...4...3...2...1...Go! Less than a minute later, Nancy was at the bottom of the course with a great time, but the second best of the day. No problem, she convinced herself. It was better to be behind, as this would get her adrenaline going and rev up her now legendary competitive drive. It was going to be like trying to beat her big sister again.

The second run was still a couple of hours away. Nancy stood around for a while with the other girls, watching the men's race. When it started to snow, the ski lodge's hot chocolate and lunch beckoned. Regardless of the pressure, Nancy could always eat. (Later she would happily endorse Mars Candy Bars.)

The second run was different and tougher than the first. Nancy found it even harder to memorize. She climbed up an exceptionally tricky section that began with a straight run but led into a sweeping turn, across a hill, and into a sudden sharp turn. This section provided

Nancy Greene on the slalom course

the perfect opportunity for a spectacular fall if she didn't approach it with care. Two of the forerunners didn't manage it and spun off course. The second racer tumbled as well, taking out a few gates. Next to go, Nancy had to be patient while the officials put the course back together. She didn't know if the skiers before her were okay, she was only told there was a "problem."

As she waited, Nancy heard the deep-voiced announcer trying to fill the time for the impatient crowds. "Nancy Greene must be very nervous at this moment," his voice boomed all over the mountain. "She has to win this race to gain the World Cup. She has to ski her best right now…" Upon hearing this, the people around Nancy at the top of the racecourse groaned. But Nancy was no longer nervous. In a breakthrough moment, she realized that she did not have to win. It wasn't going to be the end of the world if she didn't win. Later she recalled the huge knot of tension dissolving right then from her mind and her body. Skiing was supposed to be fun, and that day she had one of the best runs she'd ever made in her life.

The very fast and icy course of her second run rattled her skis but not her head. At the difficult section she had sussed out before, she glided instead of crashed. Sweeping straight to the end of the course, she crossed the finish line with an excellent time: 44:51. Was it a winning time? All she could do was wait for the others to finish.

Her biggest competitor came down a few skiers later and posted a 44:35 time. As Nancy was trying to process her apparent loss, the officials announced that they had made a mistake, reversing the last two digits of the competitor's time. This made a huge difference to Nancy when the times of the two runs were added together. Now there was only one more racer to wait for: the winner of the first run and one of the best slalom skiers on the French team. If she beat Nancy's time, then it was goodbye World Cup. For a short moment, it looked like this was going to be the case, but one little mistake on the very last part of the run made her challenger lose valuable time. Nancy Greene, the announcer boomed, had won both the race and the first-ever World Cup by less than a tenth of a second and a total of four World Cup points. Pandemonium broke out with Nancy at the centre of much laughter, hugging, and photographers' flashes. After the prizes were given out, Nancy hardly had time to join the parties because the phone in her room wouldn't stop ringing. She was the best woman skier in the world and Canada's new sweetheart.

The next year, Nancy topped her World Cup victory with Olympic medals in Grenoble, France — her third Games. She had been selected as Flag Bearer for the Canadian team as indication of how the team was counting on her for leadership. But she no longer felt

Nancy Greene at the 1968 Winter Olympics in Grenoble

the awe she had felt in her first Olympics. So much had changed. The Games were now more about sponsors and television than they were about the athletes. The sport of skiing had become more professional than amateur.

At the 1968 Games in France, Nancy had to keep up with many of the technical changes to stay competitive. She no longer taped down her baggy pants at the knee to get through the slalom gates. Instead, she wore a one-piece form-fitting racing suit. In her first race at the Grenoble Olympics, the downhill suit didn't help much as Nancy battled terrible wind and snow to place a disappointing tenth. She cried her eyes out, saying, "It was the worst disappointment of my career." Her coaches admitted later that their wax recommendation had been wrong, but Nancy refused the excuse. Nor would she complain that there hadn't been much snow for the skiers to practise on that winter. Instead, she just got "plain blazing mad" and focussed her efforts on winning the next race. Nancy came from behind in the second run of the slalom to win a silver medal.

For her final event, the coaches had to trick her with distractions, almost making her late for her turn on the course. Despite the enormous pressure, Nancy raced a remarkable giant slalom, finishing an amazing 2.64 seconds ahead of her competition and winning the gold medal. After that, her confidence knew no bounds and she scored an amazing streak of nine straight international wins, clinching her second World Cup title easily that year. During her last race, Nancy found that the challenge was gone, and the 24-year-old recognized it was time to retire. After the season was over, she travelled to France for a special victory celebration, accompanied by her sister. By that time, Liz had finished university and was well on her way to a successful career in public administration.

Nancy was ready to ski just for fun again, passing the racing poles on to younger racers inspired by her successes. In retrospect, she was certainly not sorry she had chosen skiing over skating 10 years earlier. Though she hadn't earned money while skiing as an amateur, she had pioneered new possibilities for ambitious skiers by attracting the spotlight. Chosen as the Canadian female athlete of the year (1968) and then of the century, Nancy earned over $100,000 in her first year after retirement. She ensured that part of each of her endorsement contracts benefited the whole national ski team. She also lent her knowledge and strong opinions to the government when she was asked to be part of a task force to investigate ways to help amateur athletes improve their performances. Retiring from skiing just as it was being transformed by commercial and television interests, Nancy would help guide Canada into the new reality and importance of international competitive sport.

The Tiger of the Slopes

Following in her ski tracks, thousands of young Canadians have learned to race in the Nancy Greene Ski League, which was set up by the Canadian Ski Association in 1968 to honour her successes. Betsy Clifford, Kathy Kreiner, Gerry Sorensen, Rossland neighbour Kerrin Lee-Gartner, Willy Greene Raine (Nancy's son), Kate Pace, and Melanie Turgeon have all won Olympic or World Championship titles in the years since Nancy retired. In the 1970s and 80s, Nancy's "all out" style was emulated by the Crazy Canucks. Claims Ken Read, the most famous Canuck, "Nancy influenced almost every young skier of our generation." Even today, she still loves to show her favourite ski run to people she meets on the ski lift. And she always beats them down the hill.

Epilogue

Sport is not just a game to Canadians. It means more than the score, the finish line, or the trophy; it is part of who we are and who we want to be. Our sport pioneers have helped our country find and develop its identity and individuality.

Participating and competing in sport has been an important part of Canadian life for as long as Canada has been a nation. Starting with Ned Hanlan and Tom Longboat's early days as world champions, and on to Bobbie Rosenfeld and the Grads' riding the crest of the first golden age of women in sport, Canada has celebrated its athletes as bona fide representatives of the Canadian spirit.

In the second half of the 20th century, Canada and Jackrabbit adopted each other with mutual pride, Father David Bauer made daring waves in our most Canadian of games, and "our Nancy" led Canada into the modern world of high performance international sport.

All of these athletes are symbols of our broad accomplishments. They are not part of an exclusive club, but merely a sample of Canada's rich sport history. Each pioneer also represents various segments of the Canadian mosaic: old-world immigrants, refugees, Native peoples, priests, professional men, amateur women, and the Canadian-born prodigy-next-door. These mavericks of sport opened doors for other Canadian athletes. They all left legacies far more important than what they accomplished on the track, the rink, or the racecourse. Their amazing stories will undoubtedly continue to inspire generations of Canadians.

Bibliography

Batten, Jack. *The Man Who Ran Faster Than Everyone Else.* Tundra, 2002

Cosentino, Frank. *Ned Hanlan (The Canadians).* Fitzhenry & Whiteside, 1978

Greene, Nancy with Jack Batten. *Nancy Greene: An Autobiography.* Pagurian, 1968

Hall, M. Ann. *The Girl and the Game: A History of Women's Sport in Canada.* Broadview Press, 2002

Howell, Colin. *Blood, Sweat and Cheers: Sport and the Making of Modern Canada.* University of Toronto Press, 2001

Kidd, Bruce. *The Struggle for Canadian Sport.* University of Toronto Press, 1996

Kidd, Bruce. *Tom Longboat (The Canadians).* Fitzhenry & Whiteside, 1980

Bibliography

Morrow, Don et al. *A Concise History of Sport in Canada.* Oxford University Press, 1989

Smith-Johannsen, Alice. *The Legendary Jackrabbit Johannsen.* McGill-Queen's University Press, 1993

Webb, Bernice Larson. *The Basketball Man.* University Press of Kansas, 1973

Wise, S.F. and Doug Fisher for Canada's Sports Hall of Fame. *Canada's Sporting Heroes.* General Publishing, 1974

Young, Scott. *War on Ice: Canada in International Hockey.* McClelland & Stewart, 1976

Acknowledgments

Research into the origins of hockey many years ago sparked a lifelong interest in the stories of sporting life and lives in Canada. The opportunity to share some of the fascinating stories encountered over the years has been a special pleasure.

There are many people I want to acknowledge for providing inspiration, anecdotes, and quotes for these chapters. My sporting mother, Ragnhild Dixon, not only introduced me to skiing and the sporting life, but also to the tale of her fascinating fellow Norwegian, Jackrabbit. An unpublished memoir by Terry O'Malley, one of Father David Bauer's National Team players and now a dean at Notre Dame in Saskatchewan, added much to the limited information available, and I was deeply grateful for his assistance as well as that of Father Bauer's niece, Barbara Bauer-Maison, and his close friend, Father James Hanrahan, in filling in the gaps. Nancy Greene was most generous with her help in answering questions and reviewing details in my account of her exceptional career.

Articles in Canada's History Magazine, *The Beaver*,

Acknowledgments

featuring Jackrabbit, Bobbie Rosenfeld, and Tom Longboat were engaging and helpful as were some of the entertaining journalistic accounts of the sports legends, for example, in *Great Canadian Sports Stories*, by Peter Gzowski and Trent Frayne (Canadian Centennial Publishing Co., 1965) and *Champions* by Jack Batten (NeWest, 1971). Tom Longboat was also featured in a chapter of a book of oral history, *To Run With Longboat: 12 Stories of Indian Athletes in Canada* (GMS2, 1988). With the help of Maclean's Archives, Dave Best recently compiled a new and up-to-date encyclopedia of sport, *Canada: Our Century in Sport* (Fitzhenry & Whiteside, 2002).

Two of the pioneers were also dramatically profiled in National Film Board films, *Jackrabbit* and *Shooting Stars* (the Edmonton Grads). And not to be forgotten (and certainly appreciated) are the wonderful animated resources in Canada's and Alberta's Sports Halls of Fame in Toronto and Red Deer respectively. Many thanks must go to Allan Stewart and Sandy Williams, along with their helpful staff and volunteers. Their Halls contain many more amazing stories of Canada's sporting past.

Lastly, a shower of thanks to the literary jocks in my writing life — fellow writers, readers, and editors — for "critical" encouragement all the way to the finish line.

About the Author

Joan Dixon writes from the foothills of the Rockies, where she also hikes, skis, and plays all kinds of sports with her family and friends. Her master's degree in Canadian Studies (with a specialization in sport history) and her time at the National Sport and Recreation Centre in Ottawa have helped shape her understanding of sport in Canadian life while stories of Canada and amazing Canadians have always inspired her research and writing projects. Her most recent book was *Made for Canada: the story of Avro's Arrow.*

Photo Credits

All photos are reproduced courtesy of Canada's Sports Hall of Fame

AMAZING STORIES™

EMILY CARR

The Incredible Life and Adventures
of a West Coast Artist

HISTORY/BIOGRAPHY
by Cat Klerks

Emil Carr
ISBN 1-55153-996-9

AMAZING STORIES™

NIAGARA DAREDEVILS

Thrills and Spills over the Niagara Falls

HISTORY/ADVENTURE
by Cheryl MacDonald

Niagara Daredevils
ISBN 1-55153-962-4

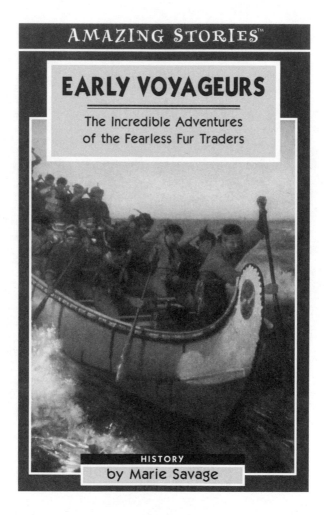

AMAZING STORIES™

EARLY VOYAGEURS

The Incredible Adventures
of the Fearless Fur Traders

HISTORY

by Marie Savage

Early Voyageurs
ISBN 1-55153-970-5

Dinosaur Hunters
ISBN 1-55153-982-9

AMAZING STORIES™

UNSUNG HEROES OF THE ROYAL CANADIAN AIR FORCE

Incredible Tales of Courage and
Daring During World War II

HISTORY
by Cynthia J. Faryon

Unsung Heroes of the Royal Canadian Air Force
ISBN 1-55153-977-2

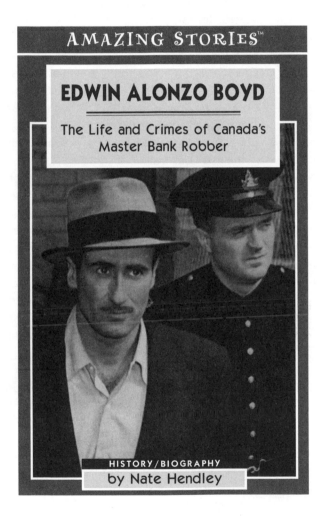

AMAZING STORIES™

EDWIN ALONZO BOYD

The Life and Crimes of Canada's
Master Bank Robber

HISTORY/BIOGRAPHY
by Nate Hendley

Edwin Alonzo Boyd
ISBN 1-55153-968-3

OTHER AMAZING STORIES

These titles are available wherever you buy books. If you have trouble finding the book you want, call the Altitude order desk at 1-800-957-6888, e-mail your request to: orderdesk@altitudepublishing.com or visit our Web site at www.amazingstories.ca

All titles retail for $9.95 Cdn or $7.95 US. (Prices subject to change.)

New AMAZING STORIES titles are published every month. If you would like more information, e-mail your name and mailing address to: amazingstories@altitudepublishing.com.